Conflict and Peacemaking in Israel-Palestine

The Israeli-Palestinian struggle is considered to be one of the most entrenched conflicts in the world. Presenting and evaluating interactive models of peacemaking and the phenomenon of intractable conflict, the book takes an in-depth look into specific models for peacemaking and applies them to the situation in Israel/Palestine.

The argument centers around the idea that a multifaceted approach to peacemaking has the greatest potential to transform an intractable conflict into a mutually beneficial social order. Encompassing theoretical background, comparative studies of conflict resolution processes in similar circumstances around the world and policy recommendations, the author presents four interactive models of peacemaking to suggest a comprehensive approach to peacemaking that attacks the conflict from various angles, directions and dimensions.

Introducing general conditions that have the potential to transform a situation of destructive conflict into a more peaceful social order, *Conflict and Peacemaking in Israel-Palestine* adds a fresh perspective to the study of destructive social conflicts and should provoke critical discussion among students and scholars of peace and conflict studies, Middle Eastern politics, conflict resolution and management.

Sapir Handelman is a visiting professor at the Center for Peace and Conflict Studies at Wayne State University, an associate at Harvard University and the Lentz Fellow in Peace and Conflict Resolution Research. His research focuses on the study of destructive social conflicts and their resolution, political theory, and applied ethics. He also leads the "Minds of Peace Experiment" at various Centers for Peace Studies around the US and the Middle East, a project which offers simulations of a potential Palestinian-Israeli public-assembly, a public negotiating congress.

Routledge Studies in Middle Eastern Politics

Conflict and Peacemaking in Israel-Palestine

Theory and Application

Sapir Handelman

LONDON AND NEW YORK

First published 2011
by Routledge
2 Park Square, Milton Park, Abingdon, Oxon OX14 4RN

Simultaneously published in the USA and Canada
by Routledge
711 Third Avenue, New York, NY 10017

Routledge is an imprint of the Taylor & Francis Group, an informa business

© 2011 Sapir Handelman

First issued in paperback 2014

The right of Sapir Handelman to be identified as author of this work has
been asserted by him in accordance with the Copyright, Designs and
Patents Act 1988.

Typeset in Times New Roman by Swales & Willis Ltd, Exeter, Devon

British Library Cataloguing in Publication Data
A catalogue record for this book is available from the British Library

Library of Congress Cataloging in Publication Data
Handelman, Sapir.
    Conflict and peacemaking in Israel-Palestine: theory and application /
    Sapir Handelman.
    p. cm.—(Routledge studies in Middle Eastern politics ; 34)
    Includes bibliographical references and index.
    1. Arab-Israeli conflict–1993– 2. Arab-Israeli conflict–1993–Peace. I. Title.
    DS119.76.H3557 2011
    956.05'4—dc22
    2010030291

ISBN: 978–0–415–49215–7 (hbk)
ISBN: 978–1–138–78023–1 (pbk)

To my beloved wife Yael and our lovely daughter Avia,
the light of our lives, who was born the same day that
I completed writing the book.

Contents

Acknowledgements

I am grateful to the Lentz Peace Research Association in St. Louis for their financial support.

Introduction

The Palestinian-Israeli struggle is an archetypical example of an intractable conflict. It is a protracted, violent, and drawn-out struggle, wherein generation after generation is socially conditioned to continue fighting. The phenomenon operates as a destructive evolutionary mechanism subject to a general principle: almost every element that benefits the conflict survives, while whatever operates against it becomes extinct. Indeed, almost every attempt to solve the Palestinian-Israeli struggle created new problems, which in turn has led to failures and regression. To stop the destructive evolutionary progression, a revolutionary process is required. The question is: How are we to design, implement, and understand such a process?

History shows that there are no simple solutions in these cases. An intractable conflict, like almost every phenomenon in the social sciences, is a "complex phenomenon."[1] This means that it is almost impossible to make specific predictions about future outcomes and to control the events in the causal chain. To put it another way, intractable conflict is likely to be influenced by so many different elements, factors, and variables that it is almost impossible to direct developments toward one specific solution. Almost any political, diplomatic, and militaristic move has unintended consequences that create new unexpected problems. Good intentions to promote peace and stability can create more harm than benefit, in the final account.

Students of social affairs, who are aware of their human limitations, can use their knowledge and expertise to search for general conditions that have the potential to minimize suffering and open opportunities to build the foundations for a peaceful social order. The art of peacemaking is to suggest a comprehensive approach to peacemaking that attacks the conflict from various angles, directions, and dimensions simultaneously, in order to create momentum for an effective peace process, which, eventually, might lead to a resolution.

This book explores the tragic phenomenon of intractable conflict and offers a multifaceted approach to peacemaking. My central claim is that a

multifaceted approach to peacemaking has the greatest potential to transform an intractable conflict into a mutually beneficial social order. This
book includes theoretical background, comparative studies of conflict resolution processes in similar circumstances around the world, and policy recommendations regarding the Palestinian-Israeli conflict itself.

I hope that this book will add a fresh perspective to the study of destructive social conflicts and that it will provoke critical and fruitful discussion
among those who are deeply engaged in, and the many more who are simply
interested in, the Palestinian-Israeli peacemaking efforts.

The Palestinian-Israeli conflict as a case study

The book, *Conflict and Peacemaking in Israel–Palestine*, emerges in the
intersection between theoretical analysis, practical examples, and policy
recommendations. I have chosen the Palestinian-Israeli conflict as my case
study, as it is one of the most complex and emotionally-fraught disputes in
the world.

The Palestinian-Israeli conflict is taking place in a tiny piece of land,
conceived as "holy" by many people around the world. This relatively
"small" conflict involves a seemingly infinite array of issues and interests,
including but not limited to: the divergent goals of three global religions;
clashes between different traditions, mentalities, and cultures; socio-
economic gaps; demographic problems; geographic barriers; civil war; and
the demand for social justice. These aspects of the conflict support my claim
that the Palestinian-Israeli struggle, like almost any intractable conflict, is a
"complex phenomenon."

The Palestinian-Israeli struggle, like a good story, has a beginning,
developments, and unexpected twists in the plot. But, unlike most great
works, it does not have an ending. Every era in the history of the struggle includes major developments and new complications that could not
have even been imagined. For example, who could expect that in 1995 an
Israeli Prime Minister would be killed by a religious Jew who was determined to stop a peace process; and who could predict that the Palestinian
people would experience a bloody civil war in 2007 that tore apart their
society.

In the Palestinian-Israeli case it seems relatively easy to identify the complexity of the conflict, which makes the resolution so elusive and difficult.
Moreover, it is a consensus among professional analysts that almost every
method of conflict resolution has been tried and failed in this desperate situation. Accordingly, I argue that the Palestinian-Israeli conflict can serve as
an excellent laboratory for the study of destructive social conflicts and the
examination of a multifaceted approach to peacemaking.

Between "conflict resolution" and "conflict management"

There are two emerging competitive trends in the extensive literature on peacemaking: conflict-management and conflict-resolution. The supporters of the conflict-management approach believe that the conflict cannot be resolved in the near future. They provide policy recommendations for improving the domestic and foreign position of each society in order to reduce the intensity of the irresolvable struggle. Hopefully, conditions for negotiation of a peace agreement will ripen in the future.[2] In contrast, the advocates of the conflict-resolution strategy argue for returning to the negotiating table to achieve a final peace agreement as soon as possible and by any means.

The arguments of the two camps sound very persuasive. The supporters of the conflict-management approach suggest that the two societies are not prepared for a serious peace process and to cope with the complications that it entails. History shows that almost any negotiating process creates dangerous and harmful side effects, such as major violent episodes carried out by the enemies of the peace process. These side effects can cause the whole process to crash, the relationships between the two societies to deteriorate, and the situation within each one of them to worsen. In the current fragile social order, it is critical to stabilize the situation and improve the position of each side before even thinking about entering into negotiations.

The supporters of the conflict-resolution approach point out that conflict-management is a poor strategy that intends to help people adjust their lifestyle to a situation of an ongoing conflict. It does not help in building the foundations for a peaceful social order. The conflict-resolution camp emphasizes that negotiations and direct interactions between the two sides are critical to understand the needs and fears of each one of them and to help in finding means to address them. Negotiations are critical to build relationships between adversaries and to give hope to the people on both sides. The lack of negotiations enables extremists, radicals, and professional spoilers to continue dictating conditions for the rest of the societies.[3]

The dispute between the two camps is not easy to reconcile. The Israeli advocates of the conflict-management approach point out that it is extremely difficult to negotiate solutions under the current situation when there is no partner for peace on the other side. The Palestinians, who lack the tradition of liberty and independence, hardly made the first steps toward establishing a well functioning state.[4] A negotiating process at this stage is only going to bring violence, frustration, and despair. Moreover, the Israeli supporters of this strategy believe that concessions to the Palestinians, who are not ready for a serious peace process, endanger the existence of Israel.

The supporters of the conflict-resolution strategy agree with the other camp that intractable conflict is a very difficult situation. They emphasize that opportunities for real substantive negotiations are very few. However, these opportunities are extremely precious and the opposing societies have to take full advantage of them. They point out that negotiating solutions, even if the process tends to collapse again and again, is the only way to stop progression in the direction of violence and destruction.

No doubt there is an amount of truth in the positions of the two camps. Moreover, it looks as if the two competitive approaches are intertwined. The reason is that it is almost impossible to manage the conflict (stabilizing the situation, reducing the level of violence, and preparing the foundations of a new social order), without addressing the main issues through direct negotiations, and vice versa. It is difficult to resolve the conflict through intensive negotiations without managing it (preparing the conditions for a new social order).

This book proposes to look at the two competitive approaches (conflict-management versus conflict-resolution) as complementary (conflict-management and conflict-resolution). In order to do this, the two approaches are regarded as much broader concepts than their traditional forms. Conflict-management is a set of strategies that are designed to build the framework for an effective peace process and to construct the foundations for a new peaceful social order. Conflict-resolution is a set of approaches intended to shape the relationships between the two societies through direct negotiations on multiple levels.

To build a comprehensive approach to peacemaking, I integrate insights from both the conflict-management and conflict-resolution approaches with lessons learned from different peacemaking strategies used in other cases of intractable conflicts. I introduce four models of peacemaking. The first, the strong-leader model, involves drastic unilateral initiatives taken by a strong leader of one of the parties. The second, the social-reformer model, encourages domestic reforms within each of the opposing societies. The third, the political-elite model, suggests traditional forms of diplomatic interaction between political elites, as the dominant peacemaking experience in the Middle East. The fourth, the public-assembly model, proposes the creation of a major Palestinian-Israeli public negotiating congress, based loosely on the multi-party talks that helped to create a dramatic change in Apartheid South Africa and in Northern Ireland during the "troubles."

I conclude that each of these models contain valuable lessons for the peacemaking efforts in the Middle East. However, no one of them can create the socio-political conditions for a long lasting peace by itself. The challenge of peacemaking is to construct a comprehensive and multidimensional approach that implements insights from each of these models simultaneously.

Four interactive models of peacemaking

The book is an initial attempt to pave the way to build, or at least to envision, a multi-dimensional approach to peacemaking. The project is to construct a comprehensive approach to peacemaking that integrates critical elements from different sources, such as various peacemaking methods, lessons from the success and failures of peacemaking initiatives, and creative ideas from the academic laboratory. As an initial stage, the main part of the book constructs, describes, and evaluates four models of peacemaking.

The *strong-leader model* involves dramatic unilateral initiatives led by a strong leader of one of the parties. This unilateral action may be political, diplomatic, or military. In general, the action is taken in order to shift the geopolitical framework of the conflict in a direction that advances a solution that the strong leader favors. Classical examples are the astonishing peacemaking trip of Anwar Sadat, the former President of Egypt, to the Israeli parliament in Jerusalem in 1977; and the unilateral withdrawal of the Israeli troops from the Gaza strip, led by the former Israeli Prime Minister Ariel Sharon, in 2005.

The first initiative led to negotiations that concluded with a peace agreement between Israel and Egypt. The second initiative did not succeed in creating a momentum for peace, to say the very least. The events that followed Sharon's unilateral initiative were civil war in Palestinian society, political division between the Palestinian leadership of Gaza and the West Bank, and escalation in the relationships between Israel and the Palestinians in Gaza.

The comparison between the two cases shows clearly that dramatic initiatives of political leaders can lead to unexpected developments. The strong-leader model proposes a desperate strategy to cope with a situation of a stalled peace process. It should be carried out with a great amount of caution after careful consideration.

The *social-reformer model* encourages domestic reforms within the opposing societies in order to build a framework for a new, peaceful, social order. Improving the socio-political conditions within Israel and the Palestinian society can help the people on both sides to discover the value of peace, motivate them to explore opportunities of how to reach it, and can invite a new peacemaking force to the stage of Middle East politics. The social-reformer model addresses the question, "How do we resolve the conflict?" by first asking, "How do we build a well functioning society in times of conflict?"

The social-reformer model draws on the free market economists' idea that an adequate framework of rules and institutions are a necessary condition for the transformation of "social chaos" to a peaceful "social order". A stable and well functioning socio-political environment is necessary to replace the destructive competition, the violent dispute, with a constructive contest, which means negotiations by peaceful means.

The social-reformer introduces domestic moves that are a pre-condition to a successful peace process, for example: improving the internal cohesion of each society, building transparent and efficient administration in the Palestinian disputed territories, reducing tensions between state and religious institutions in Israel, and providing a decent education to the people. These necessary actions have the potential to create opportunities for a reasonable peace process and reduce the political influence of extremists, radicals, and professional spoilers. In the worst-case scenario, domestic reforms help to ensure that if a peace process collapses, the results are not going to be as catastrophic as in the recent past and the opposing factions can return to the negotiation table as soon as possible.

The *political-elite model* offers various forms of interactions that can help political elites from both sides to reach understandings in a complicated situation of intractable conflict. It is the dominant peacemaking experience in Middle-East politics in general and the Palestinian-Israeli peace process in particular. The Oslo peace process of the 1990s is a classical example that can clearly demonstrate the advantages and the limitations of the political-elite model. The accord shows that the political-elite model provides effective tools for policy makers to reach agreements in a complicated situation that appears to be most desperate. However, the failure of the initiative to resolve the conflict illustrates that the model does not provide a mechanism to involve the people in the peacemaking process and prepare them for expected social crises.

The *public-assembly model* is designed to engage the people on both sides in peacemaking efforts. The model proposes the establishment of a major Palestinian-Israeli public negotiating congress. This peace-building institution invites delegations from all walks of life to discuss, debate, and negotiate solutions to their tragic struggle. It is a democratic peacemaking and peace-building institution that is designed to reflect the different opinions in the opposing societies. The public-assembly model is new in the Palestinian-Israeli experience. The vision of creating a Palestinian-Israeli public assembly is loosely based on the multi-party talks that helped to create a dramatic change in two other desperate situations of intractable conflict: Northern Ireland during the "troubles" and the struggle against Apartheid in South Africa. The political program to establish a major public negotiating congress is based on the Minds of Peace Experiment, which my colleagues and I conduct around the United States, Canada, and the Middle East.

The Minds of Peace Experiment is a small-scale Palestinian-Israeli public negotiating assembly. The exercise invites two mock-delegations of five Palestinians and five Israelis to negotiate solutions to their conflict. The formal negotiations are conducted in front of an active audience that is invited to participate in the peacemaking process. The rules of the game intend to create commitment to the negotiations, build trust, facilitate the process, and give opportunities to ordinary people to participate in the peacemaking efforts. The initiative is designed to evaluate potential outcomes of a public negotiating congress, demonstrate its peacemaking power and develop support for a potential accord.

My central argument in the book is that each of these models introduces critical elements for creating a constructive change in a situation of intractable conflict that appears to be most desperate. However, none of these models can sustain an effective peace process by itself. The art of peacemaking is to suggest a multi-faceted approach that copes with a conflict that affects almost every aspect of the social life in the opposing societies. An effective multi-faceted peacemaking approach needs to cope with different important issues in various dimensions simultaneously, for example addressing the fears and needs of the two people; preparing the conditions for a new peaceful social order; creating opportunities for negotiations between leaders; and, involving the people in the peacemaking efforts.

The four models can serve as a good introduction to cope with the challenge of peacemaking and building the foundations for a long lasting peace. My hope is that lessons driven from these peacemaking models will open a fresh perspective to the study of protracted social conflicts and their ever-elusive resolution.

The structure of the book

The book is composed of two main parts. The first provides a general background to the study as a whole, and prepares the ground for my central argument. It describes the phenomenon of intractable conflict, analyzes the case of the Palestinian-Israeli struggle, and sketches the foundations for constructing a multifaceted approach to peacemaking. The second part presents four models of peacemaking. Each model is presented in a different chapter. Each chapter begins with a theoretical background, continues with various examples, and concludes with lessons to be drawn for the peacemaking efforts in the Palestinian-Israeli case. I evaluate each model of peacemaking by exploring its risks, advantages and disadvantages. In the summary, I argue that a multifaceted approach to peacemaking that implements insights from the four models in an integrated fashion has the greatest potential to diminish destruction and to promote the ever-elusive resolution to situations of protracted social conflict. I indicate that a multifaceted approach to the study of intractable conflicts and their resolution can open a fresh perspective and lead to new discoveries in peace research.

The first part of the book sketches the landscape of the discussion and provides a general background to the study as a whole. *Chapter 1* argues that intractable conflict, like almost any phenomenon in humanities and social sciences, is a complex phenomenon. The meaning is that every social expert and professional scientist is able to understand only certain aspects of the situation according to his or her point of view and limited knowledge.[5] To demonstrate the argument, the chapter begins with two basic and fundamental questions: Why are people constantly fighting with each other? And how can conflicts be prevented, diminished, and ended?

The chapter focuses upon the theory of three prominent scholars. Each one of them explained the propensity of human beings to create misery for each other by describing social conflicts as part of an evolutionary process: Sigmund Freud, who emphasized the psycho-biological dimension; Karl Marx, who offered an economic analysis; and Samuel Huntington, who claimed that cultural differences are the root of modern conflicts.

Each of these three scholars improved our understanding of the human drive to destroy. But, none of them succeeded in providing satisfactory answers to the questions why people are constantly fighting with each other and how conflict can be eliminated. Clearly, protracted social conflicts, like the Palestinian-Israeli struggle, incorporate many dimensions of social life including those explored by Freud, Marx, and Huntington (psychology, economics, and culture). The urgent challenge of peacemaking is to construct a comprehensive approach that integrates elements from the many dimensions of our social life. To be more specific, the idea is to search for the social conditions that can maneuver the opposing people to discover the road to peaceful coexistence.

The chapter concludes by describing general patterns and symptoms that characterize the phenomenon of intractable conflict and stimulates critical thinking upon different approaches to peacemaking. It serves as an introduction to the following chapters, which claim that the Palestinian-Israeli struggle is an archetypical example of intractable conflict.

Chapter 2 provides a general background to the history and contemporary reality of the Palestinian-Israeli conflict. It traces the roots and the evolution of the conflict through exploration along three main tracks: the actual dynamic of the interaction between the two people, domestic issues within the Palestinian and the Israeli societies that have influenced their relationships, and international trends and events that shaped the conflict. The chapter introduces six major phases in the evolution of the conflict. Each phase includes unpredicted developments, new complications, and sharp twists in the melodic line of the conflict. The evolution of the struggle supports my claim that the Palestinian-Israeli struggle is a "complex phenomenon."

The chapter concludes by sketching the spectrum of the mainstream discussion upon the optimal solution to the conflict. The landscape of the discussion emerges between two extremes: "two state solution" on the one hand and "one state solution" on the other. "Two state solution" means "divorce" – a Jewish state in Israel and a Palestinian state in the West Bank and Gaza. "One state solution" means "marriage" – one democratic state for the two people. I argue that the extreme solutions are not viable options. A more realistic alternative is some kind of combination between the two extremes, for example two cooperative states under one arrangement or another.

Unfortunately, after the recent developments (the civil war in Palestinian society and the political split between Gaza and the West Bank) it is not clear anymore if the mainstream discussion ("two state solution" versus "one state solution") is relevant. The division in Palestinian society between Hamas, the radical Islamic movement that controls the Gaza strip, and the PLO (Palestine Liberation Organization), the secular nationalist party that administers the West Bank, is a major obstacle to implementing one of these solutions. This tragic development supports my claim that the focus should be upon creating the conditions necessary for building the foundations of an effective peace process. To put it differently, the challenge of peacemaking is to look for the social conditions that will help the two communities to bring creative solutions to the negotiating table.

Chapter 3 introduces the ongoing debate over the appropriate strategy to cope with the complexity of the struggle: the conflict-resolution strategy, which emphasizes the importance of negotiating a peace agreement even in difficult circumstances, and the conflict-management strategy, which eschews negotiations in favor of reducing the intensity of the irresolvable conflict to a more tolerable level, until conditions for a peace agreement are ripe.[6]

I argue that the controversy between the two competitive approaches was not created only as a result of the ongoing failures to solve the Palestinian-Israeli conflict. It is an offspring of an older dispute in international relations that started about 40 years ago. It probably began when John Burton, one of the pioneers of peace research, presented his pluralistic approach to the study of international relations, "world society", and challenged the dominant realist paradigm.[7]

In general, traditional realists interpret conflict and peacemaking in terms of interest, power struggle, and political manipulation. In contrast, pluralists suggest that the art of peacemaking is finding creative and cooperative ways to address the fears and needs of conflicting parties.[8] The chapter shows the link between the older dispute (traditional realism versus pluralism) and its modern version (conflict-management versus conflict-resolution). It presents the practical implications of the controversy upon our understanding of central motifs in peacemaking, such as negotiation. The chapter points out that the two competitive paradigms (conflict-resolution and conflict-management) should be regarded as complementary and shows how to do it.

The second part of the book presents four models of peacemaking. The first two, the strong-leader and the social-reformer, are conflict-management models, which suggest different strategies to build a framework for a new socio-political order. The last two, the political-elite and the public-assembly, are conflict-resolution models, which propose to shape the relationships between the opposing societies through direct interactions and extensive negotiations in different tracks.

The strong-leader model, which is the topic of *Chapter 4*, involves unilateral action by one of the parties to change the geopolitical structure of the conflict. In general, the action is taken by a strong leader whose domestic political control enables him or her to take drastic steps that have tremendous influence on the opposing factions and the socio-political environment. This unilateral dramatic action may be political, diplomatic, or military.

The strong-leader model is rooted in a long tradition of political thought known as the "authoritarian transition" strategy. This unusual and controversial strategy was advocated by a chain of notable scholars beginning with Niccolo Machiavelli, continued with Thomas Hobbes, and includes contemporary thinkers such as Samuel Huntington and Friedrich Hayek. These thinkers, who are well known as defenders of personal liberty, share a common belief that in desperate circumstances, where the dominant social and political experience is one of ceaseless bloodshed and strife, it is sometimes necessary to have a strong ruler wielding unchallenged authority in order to create the conditions for a peaceful and beneficial social order to emerge.[9]

The sad history of the Arab-Israeli conflict and the Palestinian-Israeli struggle provides two notable examples of unilateral actions taken by a strong leader to create a momentum for some kind of solution to the conflict: Anwar Sadat's astonishing arrival in Israel in 1977 and Ariel Sharon's unilateral withdrawal in 2005.[10] The comparison between these two "classical" cases, in addition to the theoretical foundations of the "authoritarian transition" strategy, enable me to construct the "strong-leader" model; evaluate its risks, weaknesses, and advantages; and propose policy recommendations.

Chapter 5 presents the social-reformer model, which suggests a different methodology to achieve similar objectives as those of the strong-leader model. The model offers to build the foundations of a new peaceful social environment by encouraging domestic reforms within the opposing societies. The chapter points out that chronic ambivalence in the Israeli political system and in the new emerging Palestinian authority enabled radical elements in the opposing societies to shape the geopolitical structure of the conflict and dictate conditions to the rest of the people. For example, the Israeli settlements in the disputed territories were born in a political vacuum that followed the new Israeli occupation after the 1967 war;[11] and the civil war that politically divided the Palestinian people in 2007 was the climax of political struggle between Islamic fanaticism and democratic aspirations in the disputed territories.[12]

The collapse of the Palestinian authority in 2007 is neither surprising nor astonishing. The Palestinian authority suffered from major maladies that characterized modernizing countries after World War II, as described by Samuel Huntington in 1968.[13] These examples show that a transitional period in a fragile social order can lead to social collapse and catastrophic results. One of the lessons is that major domestic reforms within the Palestinian and the Israeli societies are necessary to stabilize the situation. Moreover, following the theory of free market economists, improving the socio-political conditions within each of the opposing societies has the potential to create unintended precious opportunities for effective peacemaking initiatives. This chapter explores the domestic reforms within the Palestinian and Israeli societies, which are necessary to create the foundations of a peaceful relationship between them.

Chapter 6 presents the political-elite model. This model analyzes various forms of interaction between political elites, and is the dominant experience of the peace process as it has been conducted between Palestinians and Israelis to date. The model contains Track II diplomacy, Secret diplomacy, and Track I diplomacy.[14]

Track II diplomacy is a type of unofficial bargaining and exploration between a wide circle of influential people, who do not have an official position in the government ("mid-level elites"), for example retired politicians, academic scholars, and former senior military officers. This mode of communication intends to prepare and support the actual negotiation. Secret diplomacy is a secret negotiation between representatives of the official leadership, and aims to sketch principles to the final agreement. Track I diplomacy is the formal negotiation between official representatives of both sides where, generally, agreements are worked out.

The Oslo peace process of the 1990s is a good example of the political-elite model.[15] The accord was conducted through the various channels of the political-elite model: Track II diplomacy, Secret diplomacy, and Track I diplomacy. The chapter presents the strengths and weaknesses of the political-elite model through analysis of the achievements and failures of the Oslo process and through comparison to other diplomatic processes elsewhere. This methodology shows that the support of other peacemaking strategies can substantially improve the effectiveness of the political-elite model in practice.

Chapter 7 presents the public-assembly model, which can be viewed as complementary to the political-elite model. The political-elite model (Chapter 6) provides traditional diplomatic channels to begin a peace process, support the official negotiations, and conclude agreements between leaders. The public-assembly model (Chapter 7) provides a mechanism to involve the people in the peacemaking process through provoking a public debate in the opposing societies. The idea is to establish a major Palestinian-Israeli public negotiating congress wherein representatives of the opposing societies (Palestinian and Israeli) gather to debate, discuss, and negotiate different proposals to solve the conflict.

An efficient public negotiating congress gives political voice to different elements in the opposing societies and discourages efforts to achieve political objectives through violence. Representatives are nominated in any democratic way that can reflect the diversity of opinions in the opposing societies under one general condition – the congress excludes representatives of social and political bodies that refuse to commit to end, or at least to suspend, the violent struggle. A major public negotiating congress is a democratic peacemaking and peace-building institution, which is new to the Palestinian-Israeli experience.

The chapter proposes to establish a Palestinian-Israeli version of the all-party talks in Northern Ireland and the multi-party talks in South Africa, which were conducted during the 1990s. The chapter uses lessons from the Minds of Peace Experiment – a simulation of a Palestinian-Israeli public negotiating congress, which is conducted around the world – to explore possibilities to establish a major public negotiating congress in the Middle East and to evaluate its outcomes.

In the *Summary and conclusion*, I point out that the four models emphasize, in different ways, critical elements necessary for any effective comprehensive approach to peacemaking, for example: visionary leaders, building the foundations of a peaceful social order, negotiations between elites, and involving the people in the peacemaking process. Each of these models cannot sustain an effective peace process by itself. A multifaceted approach that uses insights from all four models is necessary to create the conditions for a constructive peace process.

I conclude that an effective peacemaking approach requires incorporating major elements from these models in an integrated fashion. My aim is to provide analysis and policy recommendations to help Palestinians and Israelis build stable relationships and discover the road to a peaceful coexistence.

Part I
General background

1 Intractable conflict as a complex phenomenon

Introduction

Intractable conflict is a protracted, destructive social situation wherein generations are born into the reality of a violent struggle. The phenomenon seems to operate as a destructive, evolutionary mechanism subject to a general rule: every element that benefits the conflict survives, while whatever operates against it becomes extinct. Indeed, almost every attempt to solve conflicts like the Palestinian-Israeli struggle creates new problems, which in turn generally lead to failure, regression, and collapse. To stop the destructive evolutionary progression, a revolutionary process is required. The question is: How to design, implement, and understand such a process?

History shows that it is extremely difficult to reach a solution in these cases. The reason is that intractable conflict, like almost every phenomenon in the social sciences, is a "complex phenomenon." This means that it is almost impossible to make specific predictions about future outcomes and to control the chain of events in the causal chain.[1] Intractable conflict is likely to be influenced by so many different factors that it is almost impossible for any human being to direct developments toward one specific solution, since there will always be unintended consequences. Any militaristic, political, and diplomatic move tends to create results, developments, and side effects that cannot be fully anticipated, predicted, and controlled.

Militaristic moves of political leaders, who believe that they are able to shape the geopolitical construction of the conflict through drastic initiatives, help to demonstrate the complexity of conflicts and the phenomenon of unintended consequences. In 1982, Ariel Sharon, the Israeli Minister of Defense, led the Israeli intervention in Lebanon. The motivation was to put an end to Palestinian insurgencies from the northern border of Israel. The Lebanon war, which was quite effective in fighting the Palestinian militias, helped to create the radical Islamist organization Hezbollah, which has proven to be one of Israel's most entrenched enemies. In 2005, Ariel Sharon, then

Prime Minister of Israel, led an Israeli unilateral withdrawal from the occupied Gaza. The events that followed this historic move, which gave hope to many Israelis, were a civil war among the Palestinians, a coup d'état of the Islamist movement Hamas, and escalation in the conflict with Israel.[2]

Intractable conflict seems to operate like a social mechanism that has a life of its own. It is similar to a disease that controls the body without any possibility to stabilize the situation. Nevertheless, there are many intractable conflicts that eventually have been resolved or, at least, transformed a dramatic change toward stability. The solutions and the road to achieve them are very different from case to case. However, the common denominator is that each former intractable conflict was considered to be a desperate situation and it took a long time and infinite change-making efforts to reach a resolution. For example, the "troubles" in Northern Ireland, an entrenched bloody conflict based on the constitutional status of a divided community, concluded with some kind of a power-sharing agreement; the struggle against the system of racial segregation in Apartheid South Africa came to a conclusion through a new democratic system; the African-American civil rights struggle in the United States succeeded in creating a social revolution which ended the codification of racism in 1965. It is almost impossible to forecast how and if the Palestinian-Israeli conflict will end one day.

The main purpose of this book is to search for general conditions that have the potential to create an effective peace process in the Middle East. True, it is almost impossible to predict specific developments in this complex situation. However, we might be able to identify general conditions and constraints that can create an environment conducive to an effective peace process. We can assume, or more precisely hope, that a comprehensive approach to peacemaking – which attacks the conflict from various dimensions, directions, and angles – has the potential to start pushing the train of peace forward.

In order to better shine a light upon the complexity of the phenomenon of intractable conflict and the challenge at stake, let me begin with a very basic and fundamental question: Why are people constantly fighting one another?

The origin of conflicts

Many scholars have tried to explain the propensity of human beings to create misery for each other and themselves. Some have attempted to find explanations by describing social conflict as part of an evolutionary process. In the modern era, this scholarly endeavor includes prominent intellectuals such as Sigmund Freud, who focused on the psycho-biological dimension; Karl Marx, who offered an economic analysis; and Samuel

Huntington, who spoke about the clash of civilizations, and suggested a cultural explanation.

In 1932, Albert Einstein invited Sigmund Freud to exchange views on the question: "Is there any way of delivering mankind from the menace of war?" Freud's answer became a well-known composition entitled "Why war?".[3]

In his thoughtful answer Freud described the history of humanity as an evolutionary interplay between two opposing compulsions in human nature: erotic and death. The first is a strong drive to create while the other is a powerful need to destroy. These two competitive forces are operating side by side. One manifestation of this phenomenon is that almost any positive development and elaboration in human life also has destructive components. For example, the development of science has also enabled sophisticated production of weapons of mass destruction. Scientists, who are supposed to improve our knowledge and quality of life, as Professor Agassi (1985) noted, became a leading powerful force in the arms race. The questions are: Is the death instinct the source of all conflicts? Can it be that humankind is destined to progress from one conflict to another? What can we do in order to change, or at least to transform or moderate, our death instinct? Can it be that the actual source of the Palestinian-Israeli struggle is damage in human production?

It is difficult to argue with Freud about the inherent propensity of human beings to destroy, especially if we observe the Palestinian-Israeli conflict. The two communities constantly operate against their best interests and show, quite effectively, their ability to create misery for each other. However, Freud does not help us in finding solutions to this tragic struggle. In regard to specific urgent cases of conflict, Freud recommends continued implementation of the peacemaking methods that are familiar to us.[4] Unfortunately, peacemaking strategies familiar and available to us have not succeeded, so far, in bringing about a peaceful resolution to the Palestinian-Israeli struggle.

Freud sketches guidelines for a master program that can lead to a better world. He emphasizes the importance to restrain the death instinct by strengthening its counterpart the erotic compulsion. He recommends the following measures: increasing positive sentiments and identification between human beings,[5] developing knowledge that can help us control our destructive instincts, and creating public institutions of independent thinkers that can guide the masses.[6] However, the question of how to build the foundations of an effective peace process in desperate situations of intractable conflicts, like the Palestinian-Israeli struggle, remains an enigma.

In his evolutionary journey, Freud comes to a conclusion that almost any social order, even under the rule of law, is not going to be stable. One of the reasons is the inevitable tension and struggle between two major classes: the rulers and the ruled. The elite always try to expand their authority and to put themselves above the law, while the ruled struggle for more rights.[7] The Palestinian-Israeli conflict demonstrates that this observation, or maybe general pattern of conduct, is not always accurate. For example, one of the symptoms of the Palestinian-Israeli conflict is that any progress toward a peaceful resolution of the struggle, a resolution that intends to put an end to the occupation and the division between rulers ("the Israeli occupiers") and the ruled ("the Palestinians occupied"), tends to increase the level of violence from both sides (the "occupier" and the "occupied"). From the Oslo Accord of the 1990s to Ariel Sharon's unilateral disengagement in 2005 almost any substantial move – political, diplomatic, or militaristic – toward some kind of resolution ended with fallbacks, violence, and despair.

Freud's explanation of the origin of conflicts, the death instinct, taught us something about the nature of human beings. However, it does not provide any specific guidelines to cope with the urgent needs of Palestinians and Israelis to restrain their destructive compulsion and start promoting the culture of peace in a constructive way that can put an end to their struggle.

Our next evolutionary theory in our exploration of the origins of conflict is Karl Marx's theory of social change. Marx, like Freud, points out that class struggle is a major cause for instability in almost any social order.[8] However, the emphasis is different. Freud emphasizes the psychological dimension while Marx underlines the economic sphere. According to Freud, any kind of conflict is a different manifestation of the interplay between two basic instincts – erotic and death – while according to Marx, the development of material means of production enfolds the evolutionary history of struggles.

According to Marx, the capitalist system, the latest phase in social development, is inherently built to increase wealth and misery simultaneously. The development, elaboration, and accumulation of the means of production tend to increase the productivity of work and create intolerable gaps between the ruling class and the ruled. The rich become richer, the poor become poorer, and the middle class tends to vanish.[9] The tensions between the two major classes (the rulers and the ruled) lead to clashes and, eventually, to revolution.[10]

There is no need to be an expert in Marxist theory to notice the economic gaps between the Israeli society and the Palestinian one. These gaps create tensions that are manifested in many different ways. Moreover, the Israelis have succeeded in adjusting their economy to major crises that result from the conflict, such as the *Intifada* (the spontaneous uprising of the Palestinians) and the ongoing closures that prevent Palestinian workers from coming to work in Israel. Israelis have altered and developed their means of production in many different ways, for example developing advanced high technological industry and using foreign workers to replace the Palestinians. In contrast, the Palestinians face major difficulties in starting to build a viable economy in most of the territories of Gaza and the West Bank.

Marxist theory is considered to be an important benchmark in western thinking. For example, the economic dimension took a central place in the study of war and peace in modernizing theories in the period between 1940 and 1960.[11] However, the emphasis of Marx and modernizing theories is different. Marx saw in economic development a source of instability in capitalist societies (increase the gaps between classes) while developing theories pointed out that economic progress is a peacemaking power that can produce stability in modernizing societies.[12]

Modernizing theories emphasize that economic development is the main foundation for progress in the many other dimensions of social life: it stimulates the development of knowledge (research and development), creates the conditions for better education, reduces poverty, and promote liberal values such as freedom, independence, and responsibility.[13] Huntington, in his famous book *Political Order in Changing Societies* (1968) turned this conventional wisdom on its head.

Huntington argued that economic development without political reforms cannot bring stability in modernizing countries. A pre-condition for a stable social order is first and foremost an adequate framework of a legal system and political institutions and not necessarily economic progress. He points out that there are unstable countries with modern economies and there are stable countries with backward economies.[14]

There are many examples in the history of conflicts and peacemaking in the Middle East and the international arena that can demonstrate Huntington's arguments: the collapse of the Palestinian authority in 2007 (following the Israeli unilateral withdrawal from the Gaza strip) was mainly due to an unstable political system and not because of a failed economy; there is an economic boom in Ramallah, the unofficial capital of the West Bank, which can quite easily collapse because of an unstable political system and lack of progress in the peace process;[15] and the protracted conflicts in Northern Ireland and South Africa have undergone a dramatic change toward stability, despite major economic problems.[16]

There is no doubt that economics plays an important role in conflict and peacemaking. However, the direction of influence is not always clear. Economic development can promote political stability and can create dangerous political tensions.[17] The crucial point is that economic considerations alone cannot provide satisfactory answers to the general question of why people are fighting and to the specific riddle of how to promote peace in the Palestinian-Israeli situation.

Our next station in the journey to trace the origins of conflicts is Samuel Huntington's highly controversial theory – "the clash of civilizations." Huntington, who challenged the conventional wisdom in 1968 and demonstrated that political reforms are critical to promote peace and stability in developing countries, argued in 1993 that the cultural dimension of our social life contains an adequate explanation for the origins of modern conflicts.[18]

Huntington describes the development of the modern western world (Western civilization) through the evolution of conflicts: conflicts between princes turned into struggles among nations, which yielded to the clashes of ideologies. The next phase in the evolution of conflicts, which we begin to experience in our days, is the clash between the different civilizations.[19]

A civilization, according to Huntington, is a cultural unit. It is an entity that unites different individuals, groups, and communities under the same broad cultural identity, for example, Arab, Chinese, and Western civilizations.[20] In these terms, we can identify the Palestinian-Israeli conflict as a manifestation of inevitable clashes between the Jewish and the Arab civilizations.

No doubt that Jews and Arabs have major differences in their culture, mentality and tradition. These differences can create tensions in their interactions, especially, if they are living side by side. However, "globalizing" the Palestinian-Israeli conflict and presenting it as a manifestation of clashes between different civilizations is complicating the situation in a way that it will be almost impossible even to start thinking "how to solve the conflict?" In contrast, "localizing" the conflict and viewing it as a struggle between two communities, Israelis and Palestinians, who are destined to live together has a better chance in helping the opposing societies discover peace. This is the approach of this book.

The prima facie simplification, or more precisely generalization, of the conflict – struggle between the Jewish civilization and the Arab one – ignores major tensions in Palestinian society. The question of identity (national, cultural, or both) is a major factor that led to a political split in Palestinian society (Gaza and the West Bank). The violent struggle between the PLO, the secular nationalist movement, and Hamas, the Islamist group, who probably strive for the revival of the Islamic civilization,[21] led to a tragic civil war that ended, so far, with a political division between the West Bank (under PLO control) and Gaza (under the Hamas leadership).[22]

In general, culture can play a major role in conflict and peacemaking. However, its degree of influence is highly controversial and the direction of its impact (conflict or peacemaking) is not always clear. Freud, for example, emphasizes the peacemaking potential of cultural development while Huntington emphasizes the destructive impact of cultural differences.

Freud claims that cultural development is a major element that can help in reducing the amount of wars. Cultural development enables us to better control, monitor, and restrain the destructive compulsions and instincts of human beings.[23] In contrast, Huntington points out that cultural development within each civilization operates in the other direction, at least in our era. It increases and develops sentiments of distinct cultural identity within each civilization and creates tensions and conflicts between them. The philosopher Karl Popper would probably claim that there is an amount of truth in both positions. The impact of culture, destructive or constructive, depends on the circumstances and the interplay of other factors and variables.

Popper claims that assembling the complexity of social phenomenon into one dimension (psychology, economics, or culture) is a problematic simplification: Freud's mistake was the belief that the very essence of almost any social phenomenon is psychological; Marx's error was the focus on the economic dimension as the source of almost any human problem;[24] we can add and assert that Huntington's inaccuracy was to claim that the nature of modern conflict is cultural.

There is no doubt that Freud, Marx, and Huntington have contributed valuable insights that have expanded our understanding of the human will to destroy. Nevertheless, none of them succeeded in providing a satisfactory answer to the persistent riddle: How can conflicts be prevented, and how can they be ended?

Clearly, conflicts are not simple; even the smallest disagreements can reach almost infinite complexity, incorporating all of the dimensions explored by Freud, Marx, and Huntington. The urgent challenge of peacemaking requires a comprehensive approach that incorporated the many aspects of our social life in an integrated fashion. The tragic phenomenon of intractable conflict can quite easily demonstrate this urgent need.

Intractable conflict as a complex phenomenon

Intractable conflict, is a widespread phenomenon in the contemporary world. What is so astonishing is that human beings are able and willing to cause so much destruction over a long period of time, even when doing so contradicts their own best interests, preferences, and priorities. In classical examples of intractable conflicts, like the Palestinian-Israeli case, any progression toward resolution leads to an increase in the level of violence.[25] The results are, usually, regression, despair, and, even, escalation.

Protracted conflicts often begin with "real problems" (not everything is only psychology). "Real problems" are problems that in principle can be quantified, manageable, and in an ideal world could be, probably, resolved by a reasonable compromise. Examples of "real problems" could be: territorial claims, disputes over allocation of resources, and demographic complications. However, in our real human world the subjective dimension (the mental sphere) complicates the situation beyond any possible imagination.

The mental factor reveals its presence in the commonality and the diversity between the societal elements that are involved in the struggle. The commonality is expressed in psychological conditions that society's members tend to develop in times of intractable conflict and facilitate its continuation. The diversity and differences between the various agents within each side can be a major obstacle for building the foundations of a peaceful social order. Let me elaborate on those two levels of complication.

People involved in protracted conflicts have a propensity to share entrenched beliefs and accumulate animosity and prejudice that manifests in classical symptoms, such as: survival – the people in each of the opposing parties believe that existential issues are at stake; mirror image – each side believes that the rival is not interested in peace;[26] and victimhood – each side believes that they are the victim in the current situation or, at least, going to be the victim in a new social order.[27] These societal beliefs and entrenched conventions – whether they are realistic, half realistic, or complete fantasy – help to perpetuate the conflict. Moreover, they prepare the ground for radicals, extremists, and professional spoilers – societal elements that object any progression toward reasonable resolution and make all efforts to stop any peacemaking process – to dictate conditions for the rest of the people.

Despite the belief that people involved in protracted conflict share, human beings are, still, different from one another. Each of the opposing parties is a composite of various societal elements, such as individuals, groups, and communities. It is almost impossible to find a compromise that is going to satisfy everyone. The result is that any progress toward peace, or at least toward a new social order, exposes diversities, adversaries and tensions within the opposing factions. Societies that lack political mechanisms to resolve disputes by peaceful means can quite easily, in a transitional period, experience domestic violence, collapse into chaos and develop new severe crises.[28] For example, in 2007, following the Israeli unilateral withdrawal from Gaza, a bloody civil war erupted amongst the Palestinian people that politically divided their society; in South Africa, around the time of the dismantling of the Apartheid system and the construction of a new social order, violent clashes erupted between different ethnic groups within the "black" camp.[29]

The focus on the mental factor (communality and diversity within each of the opposing societies) and the complication that it creates helps to draw only part of the picture. The reason is that it does not give much attention to many elements, components, and variables that, directly and indirectly, play a significant part in intractable conflicts, for example: the influence of external players (such as, US, Iran, and the Arab League in the Palestinian-Israeli case), the efficiency of the political system within each of the opposing sides, education, economic development, knowledge, and the impact of spoilers.

To improve the picture, it could be useful to add an additional angle of vision and point out that protracted conflicts are influenced by factors and variables in three main levels: the relationship between the opposing parties (Palestinians versus Israelis); domestic issues within each of the opposing parties (such as tensions, disagreements, and political barriers within the Palestinian and Israeli societies); impact of international players, global trends, and major events (for example, the rise and decline of Arab nationalism, the Cold War and its aftermath, the rise of political Islam and the Holocaust).[30]

One of the symptoms of intractable conflict is that a major portion of the people involved in the struggle are exhausted, tired, and about to lose their patience. The climax of "conflict fatigue" is a breaking point. A breaking point can lead to resolution or escalation and transformation. For example, the Omagh bombing on August 15, 1998, where almost 220 people were injured and 29 people were killed, is considered the event that concluded the "troubles" in Northern Ireland. The people in Northern Ireland stopped letting extremists dictate conditions for them.[31] In contrast, a car accident on December 9, 1987 was the fuse that lit the first *Intifada*, the spontaneous uprising of the Palestinian people in the disputed territories.[32] It was the beginning of a new chapter in the bloody history of the Palestinian-Israeli struggle. Gaza and the West Bank became the focal point of the struggle[33] and the radical Islamist movement Hamas, a militant outgrowth of the Muslim Brotherhood, was born.[34]

It is almost impossible to predict future developments even when intractable conflict is getting close to, or has already reached, a breaking point. The direction of progress depends on many variables and factors that could not be summarized in a set of mathematical equations. Among the elements that determine the outcomes are: the preparation of the opposing societies for a new social order, the availability of peacemaking and peace-building strategies, the impact of political leaders, the influence of international players, and the functioning of political institutions.

Our limitations in analyzing and predicting future developments and implications of intractable conflicts point to the paradoxical feature of this section. The purpose here is to simplify the phenomenon of intractable conflict in order to explain and demonstrate its complexity. Any human being, a including social expert, can only grasp and understand certain aspects of intractable conflicts and is only able to describe the phenomenon from his or her particular point of view.[35] Nevertheless, there is consensus among social experts upon general broad characteristics of intractable conflict that could demonstrate the complexity of the phenomenon:[36]

- *Protracted* – Intractable conflicts are long-time struggles wherein generations in turn experience violent clashes.
- *Irresolvable* – The conventional wisdom among those involved in intractable conflicts is that the struggle cannot be resolved.
- *Existential* – Parties involved in intractable conflicts believe that it is a struggle for their survival.
- *Central* – Intractable conflicts affect almost any aspect of social life in the opposing societies.

In addition, it is possible to add the following characteristics:

- *Extremists* – often enough, extremists dictate conditions for the rest of the people. — Hamas
- *Complications* – almost any progression toward resolution of the conflict leads to: an increase in the level of violence, transformation, and unexpected complications.
- *Fatigue* – Most members of the conflicting parties are exhausted and tired of the struggle.
- *Complexity* – Intractable conflict is a complex phenomenon.

The tragic history of intractable conflicts shows that reaching a peace agreement between leaders and political elites is usually not enough to stop the struggle. There is an urgent necessity to create the conditions for an effective peace process and build the foundations of a peaceful social order. The challenge of peacemaking is to suggest and implement a multifaceted approach that attacks the conflict from various angles, directions, and dimensions simultaneously.

2   The Palestinian-Israeli conflict

Introduction

The Palestinian-Israeli conflict is considered to be one of the most entrenched conflicts in the world. It is a struggle between two people over a tiny piece of land that is conceived as holy by major actors who have a stake in the struggle. This relatively small conflict involves an almost infinite array of issues and interests, including but not limited to: the divergent goals of three global religions; clashes between different traditions, mentalities, and cultures; socio economic gaps; demographic problems; civil war; and the demand for social justice.

These aspects of the conflict clearly indicate that the Palestinian-Israeli struggle, like almost any intractable conflict, is a "complex phenomenon." Despite the complexity of the situation, which far exceeds the imagination, there is a clear international consensus about the optimal solution. The principle is two states for the two communities ("two state solution"): an Israeli state and an independent Palestinian state in the West Bank and Gaza. The question that analysts have been struggling with for almost 30 years is: How to reach the consensus solution?

The purpose of this book is not to present, analyze, and evaluate different solutions to the conflict. The main focus is to sketch guidelines for an effective peace process that can invite different solutions and creative ideas to the negotiation table. The approach here is to search for the social conditions that can help, motivate, and maneuver the opposing societies to discover the road to peaceful coexistence. Nevertheless, the consensus solution and its consolidation, whether it is viable or not, can help us in tracing the evolution of the conflict.

It is quite clear that history can be presented in many different ways. Moreover, in almost any intractable conflict, like the Palestinian-Israeli case, the opposing factions tend to develop different and, even, contradictory narratives. Each side of an incomputable historical narrative can appear well constructed, reasonable, and have its own appeal.[1] Ironically, there is usually an amount of truth in each one of them. Unfortunately, it is almost impossible to determine to what extent each of the opposing sides is right or wrong, and to translate it to practical measures that are going to bring peace and stability. This is one of the reasons that effective and efficient negotiations should avoid historical debate, as much as possible.[2]

This book proposes to look at an effective peace process as a pragmatic search for practical solutions to the urgent problems at stake. The focus is upon building the conditions that can engage the opposing societies in a joint search for improving the present situation and building a better future. The main purpose of this chapter is to provide a brief historical overview of the conflict and to sketch the spectrum of the discussion on possible solutions.[3]

The evolution of the Palestinian-Israeli conflict: a brief overview

The history of the Palestinian-Israeli struggle is structured like a work of modern art. It includes plot elements of a best seller: introduction, development, drama, tension, hopes, disappointments, and many unexpected twists along the way. However, unlike most works of art, the Palestinian-Israeli conflict does not yet have an ending.

Introduction: the political struggle over the future of Palestine (1897–1947)

The first Zionist congress, which was held in Basel in 1897, is considered by historians as the beginning of the Palestinian-Israeli struggle.[4] The Jewish Zionists came to the conclusion that the only solution to the "Jewish problem" – putting an end to a tragic history of discrimination, oppression and persecution – was to establish a state for the Jewish people in the historic homeland.[5] The goal became "to create for the Jewish people a home in Palestine secured by public law." The political program was to purchase land in Palestine – which was mostly swampy, marshland, and uninhabited – to cultivate it, and to turn it into a flourishing garden.[6]

The birth of political Zionism in the beginning of the twentieth century brought waves of Jewish immigrants who built settlements, established political and social institutions, and began to create the foundations of a new state. The growing Jewish presence in Palestine created tensions with the local Arab population who had their own expectations for independence.[7] The violence between the two communities in Palestine, Jewish and Arab, began in the 1920s and has not stopped.

Both communities understood that controlling the land meant political power. However, subsequent international trends and global events have shaped the relationships between the Jewish and the Arab communities in Palestine. The rise of Arab nationalism as a reaction to Turkish imperialism and western colonialism turned the problem of Palestine into an Arab problem (not only a Palestinian one).[8] The growing Anti-Semitism in Europe, which culminated with the Holocaust, increased Jewish immigration into Palestine and put the necessity to find an appropriate accommodation for Jewish refugees on the agenda of the international community.

Following the Holocaust, in November 1947, the United Nations General Assembly voted to end the British mandate over Palestine and divided the western part of the land between a Jewish and Arab state. The Jewish leadership in Palestine accepted the partition plan with reservations, while the Arab leadership, within and outside Palestine, rejected it.

On May 15, 1948, after the British forces pulled out, the Jewish leadership in Palestine declared the establishment of the independent state of Israel. Unfortunately, the happiest date for Jewish Israelis is marked as a traumatic event in the Palestinian calendar. The anniversary day of independence for Israelis became the day of the catastrophe (the Nakba Day) for Palestinians. However, the "liberation" of Palestine remained an Arab nationalist mission.

Internationalization – the Arab-Israeli conflict (1947–67)

Following the Israeli Declaration of Independence on May 15, 1948, Arab armies invaded Israel and a full-scale war erupted between Israel and its neighboring Arab countries. The local and communal struggle between Arab and Jewish residents of Palestine was officially transformed into a broad Arab-Israeli conflict.

The new Israeli Defense Forces (IDF) succeeded in defending the emerging Jewish state and Israel increased its portion of western Palestine by 20 percent. In July of 1949 an armistice line agreement was signed between Israel and the neighboring Arab countries. The focal point of the Palestinian-Israeli struggle today, Gaza and the West Bank, remained under Arab control; the West Bank was annexed by Jordan and the Gaza strip was administered by Egypt. The cease-fire line became the official border of Israel until the Six-Day War of 1967. The internationalization of the Palestinian-Israeli conflict manifested itself in two dimensions: the emergence of the Palestinian refugee problem and the rise of pan-Arabism which exacerbated the determination of the Arab state to take revenge and dismantle the Jewish state.

The 1948 war created about 725,000 Palestinian refugees who spread out in the region. Two competitive narratives were developed to explain this tragic result. The Israeli narrative suggests that the Arab refugees left their homes of their own free will in order to facilitate the destruction of the Jewish state by the regular Arab armies. The Palestinian narrative suggests that the Arab refugees were simply deported by the Israelis. It is hard to reconcile the two competitive hypotheses and, there probably is an amount of truth in each one of them. However, it is clear that in any negotiation about the future of the region, the Palestinians will demand a solution to the refugee problem.[9]

The second dimension that broadly manifested over the future of Palestine was the rise of Arab nationalism. The movement reached its peak with the emergence of the charismatic leader Gamal Abdel Nasser, who took control as President of Egypt in 1954. Nasser became the champion of pan-Arabism, which means that all Arabs belong to one nation though they may residence in different countries.[10] The Palestinians are an integral part of the greater Arab nation and do not have a distinct national identity.

Nasser's aspirations were to create a united Arab world that could compete with the west and eliminate its influence. The existence of a Jewish western state on what he considered to be Arab soil was regarded as part of western colonialism. The climax of the violent clashes between Israel and the Arab world in general, and Israel and Egypt in particular, was the Six-Day War of 1967. However, instead of fulfilling Nasser's aspirations to eradicate the Jewish state, one of the main results of the war was the collapse of the pan-Arabism dream.

Communalization – Palestinization of the Arab-Israeli conflict (1967–79)

The results of the 1967 war dramatically changed the geopolitical structure of the Arab-Israeli conflict. Israel took control over Gaza and the West Bank and created more defensible borders in the north and the south by occupying the Golan Heights and Sinai Peninsula from Syria and Egypt respectively. However, the Palestinians once again became the central players in the confrontation.

As Herbert Kelman, who coined the term Palestinization of the Arab-Israeli conflict, noted, the main conflict once again became between Israelis and Palestinians who have territorial claims over the same tiny piece of land.[11] The main reasons that led to the Palestinization of the Arab-Israeli conflict are: the inability of the Arab states to defeat Israel; the lack of commitment of Arab leaders to fight for Palestinian objectives; the reluctance of the Arab leaders to help in finding solutions to the humanitarian problems of the refugees; and, the collapse of the Pan-Arabism dream, at least in the form that Nasser envisioned.[12]

Although the PLO, which was created by the Arab League in 1964 for various political reasons, was supposed to lead the struggle over Palestine, the Palestinians began to understand that they have to take their fate in their own hands. Indeed, it was the Fatah which became the primary Palestinian organization. The Fatah, which was founded by a group of Palestinian students in Cairo in the late 1950s, eventually took over the PLO in 1969 and Yasser Arafat became its chairman and leader.

The new occupation of Gaza and the West Bank gave Israel more defensible borders and better opportunities to fight Palestinian insurgencies. However, Israel faced a major challenge to its democracy. Following the new reality, approximately 1,200,000 Palestinians were living under military occupation by a state that is considered to be the only democratic country in the region (with the possible exception of Turkey).

The climax of the Palestinization of the Arab-Israeli conflict was the peace treaty between Israel and the strongest Arab country, Egypt, in 1979. Anwar Sadat, the successor of Gamal Abdel Nasser as the President of Egypt, launched a diplomatic offensive on Israel by coming to speak peace in the Israeli parliament in 1979. This sophisticated peacemaking move enabled Sadat to reach major objectives, such as recovering the Sinai Desert, that he failed to achieve in the October War of 1973. However, after desperate attempts to negotiate for the Palestinian goals, the President deserted the Palestinians. Jewish settlements in the territories continued to appear, grow, and expand.[13]

Assembling – Gaza and the West Bank become the focal point (1979–91)

The Palestinian-Israeli conflict gradually shifted its emphasis from aspirations to "liberate" Palestine to establishing an independent state in Gaza and the West Bank. The Palestinians began to accept the fact that it would be impossible for them to dismantle the Jewish state. The PLO gradually changed its agenda from territorial claims over the whole area of mandatory Palestine (including Transjordan – "we must liberate Amman before we liberate Tel-Aviv")[14] through a militant struggle over the western part of the land ("driving the Jews into the sea") to the struggle for an independent state in Gaza and the West Bank.[15]

The Israelis from their side began to understand that the Palestinians in the territories were not going to vanish. The occupation has sharpened the tensions between the Jewish and democratic features of the state that have been present since its establishment.[16] On the one hand, granting citizenship to the Palestinians in the territories was perceived as a threat to the Jewish character of the country. However, on the other hand, maintaining a military occupation in the territories, over about 1,200,000 people, is not in tune with the spirit of democracy. Unfortunately, the Israeli leadership did not have a clear political strategy to cope with this complicated situation. The settlement project, the establishment of Jewish settlements in the disputed territories, was born in this political vacuum. The project which was initiated to fulfill specific strategic needs, grew and transformed into an instrument to implement the ideology of greater Israel. The Jewish settlements created facts on the ground that have to be seriously considered in any negotiations that intend to bring a solution to the Palestinian-Israeli struggle.[17]

The PLO led the militaristic struggle through insurgencies against Israelis within the state of Israel and abroad. The PLO's armed forces were forced to wander from place to place. They were deported from Jordan to Lebanon in 1971 ("Black September"), dispersed to eight different countries following the Israeli invasion to Lebanon in 1982 (the First Lebanon war), and, finally, Arafat established his headquarters in Tunis.

Another turning point in the struggle was the breakout of the first *Intifada*, the spontaneous uprising of the Palestinian people in the territories in 1987, which caught almost everyone who was involved in the conflict by surprise. The *Intifada*, which "officially" put Gaza and the West Bank in the center of the struggle, demonstrated to the Israelis that they were dealing with the national sentiments of people that could not be suppressed by military force. However, the Palestinians needed a political strategy to translate a spontaneous revolt into political achievements. It was an opportunity for Arafat, who so effectively used violent means to attract attention to the Palestinian problem,[18] to change his tactics. Arafat shifted the emphasis from violent struggle to political and diplomatic initiatives. He searched for political solutions to the struggle that would enable him to retain his position as the ultimate leader of the Palestinian people. Not everyone in Palestinian society saw it in a good light. The first *Intifada* showed clear signs of a bitter leadership struggle in Palestinian society. The *Intifada* was the catalyst for the establishment of Hamas, a militant outgrowth of the Muslim Brotherhood. The establishment of Hamas was a radical shift in the tactic of the Brotherhood to achieve its objectives.

The Muslim Brotherhood started its operation in the Holy Land in 1947. Their activities focused mainly upon building the foundations of Islamic state through charity organizations, religious institutions, social clubs, and Islamic education. In general, the Brotherhood refrained from active resistance to the Israeli occupation in the West Bank and Gaza and focused upon building the foundations for an Islamic revolution.

The growing national sentiments of the Palestinians reached its peak during the first *Intifada*, and made the leadership of the Brotherhood consider changing their policy. They began to understand that in order to maintain popularity and supporters, they needed to start taking an active part in the violent struggle. The result was the establishment of Hamas, a militant out-growth of the Brotherhood.[19]

The two main competitive movements in Palestinian society, the PLO and Hamas, developed different political agendas. The primary goal of the mainstream in the PLO was to establish an independent state in Gaza and the West Bank. In contrast, the ideologists of Hamas saw in any compromise with Israel a religious sin. They are committed to establish an Islamic autoc-racy in all of Mandatory Palestine, which they view as an Islamic property.

The leadership of the PLO began to understand the importance of peace-ful negotiation with Israel to achieve their political goal. However, inter-national pressure was needed to begin a new phase in the history of the Palestinian-Israeli struggle.

Peacemaking – The rise of the "two state solution" (1991–2000)

The end of the cold war created new opportunities for peacemaking in the Middle East. The relationships between Israel and the PLO gradually shifted from political detachment (Madrid conference in 1991) through indirect negotiations that resulted in mutual recognition (the Oslo peace process in 1993) to commitments by the leadership for a "two state solution" (Annapo-lis summit of 2007).

In the aftermath of the First Gulf War of 1991, the United States admin-istration, under President George Bush, was determined to take a central role in the creation of a "new" Middle East. The administration called for an international conference for comprehensive peace in the Middle East in Madrid. The Madrid conference included multilateral talks with broad par-ticipation (such as representatives of European countries, China, and Japan) and bilateral talks between Israel and the neighboring Arab countries. The compromise that enabled the participation of a reluctant hard-line Israeli government, under Prime Minister Yitzhak Shamir, was a joint Jordanian-Palestinian delegation which does not officially include PLO members and Palestinians from East Jerusalem.

The Madrid conference and the subsequent negotiations in Washington were far from reaching agreements that could lead to a new peaceful Middle East. However, it was an important initiative that brought the leadership of Israel and the Arab countries to the negotiation table. It was the beginning of a new peacemaking process and no one could predict its future.

The deteriorating situations in the territories and high cost of the *Inti-fada* led to growing support within the Israeli public for moving forward in the negotiations. The result was a shift in the Israeli general elections that brought Yitzhak Rabin, the leader of the Labor party, to the Prime Minister's office. Rabin was elected based on the belief that he was the only leader that could reach an agreement with the Palestinians. Indeed, Rabin promised the Israeli voters to reach an autonomy agreement with the Palestinians within six to nine months after the general elections in Israel.[20] However, the negotiations in Washington (following Madrid) did not show any signs of progress.

Arafat was also in a difficult situation: he was in exile; he could not participate in the official negotiations in Washington (the PLO was considered to be a terrorist organization by Israel and the United States); the PLO lost funding from the Gulf States because of Arafat's support of Saddam Hussein during the Gulf crises; Hamas and the other Islamist extremist groups, the PLO competitors, became more and more popular in the territories. In short, the two leaders, Rabin and Arafat, desperately needed a dramatic breakthrough for their own political survival.

Parallel to the stalled official negotiations in Washington, a secret unofficial engagement opened in Oslo in 1992. Two Israeli academics met low rank PLO officials in order to explore possibilities toward resolving the Palestinian-Israeli struggle. It was a precious opportunity for the two leaders, Rabin and Arafat, to negotiate indirectly and to test each other's ability, willingness, and seriousness to reach and deliver an effective peace agreement.[21]

The Oslo Accord, which is considered to be the most significant peace initiative between 1977 and 2005, was finalized in Washington in 1993 with mutual recognition between Israel and the PLO. The accord enabled Arafat and his people to go back to the territories and begin to establish "a Palestinian Interim Self Government Authority." It was agreed that the transitional period would not exceed five years; negotiations, between "the Government of Israel and the Palestinian people's representatives," on a permanent solution would start no later than "the beginning of the third year of the interim period."[22] The idea of establishing an independent Palestinian state in Gaza and the West Bank was not mentioned in the Oslo agreement. However, it was clear, at least to the Palestinians, that the accord was an important milestone toward the implementation of a "two state solution."

Unfortunately, the two people, Israelis and Palestinians, were not ready and prepared to face the difficulties, obstacles, and expected crises that any serious peacemaking process entails. Following the accord the political situation was teetering from one crisis to another: *leadership* – Rabin, the Israeli Prime Minister, was assassinated by an Israeli Jewish extremist; *administration* – the new Palestinian authority was suffering from major maladies of developing countries, such as blatant corruption and dysfunction of the governing system; *extremists* – the enemies of the peace process kept the violent struggle alive: suicide bombers frequently blew themselves up within Israel and the settlement project continued to grow in the Palestinian territories.

The political systems of both sides showed severe symptoms and signs of desperation. The Arafat administration gave the impression that they were losing control and were unable to determine the political agenda of the Palestinians. The Israeli leadership was swinging between the right-wing government of Benjamin Netanyahu (1996–99) and the left-wing government of Ehud Barak (1999–2001). The instability reflected the confusion and the growing despair among the public on both sides.

In late September 2000, following the second Camp David summit, which concluded infinite attempts to find peaceful solutions to the conflict, a new *Intifada* broke out. The peace process was officially collapsing into another violent cycle.

Split – the triple conflict – Israel, Gaza, and the West Bank (2000–the present)

The collapse of the peace process led to increased ambiguity, growing instability, and ironic paradoxes. The swing between the right and left in Israeli politics reached its peak with the election of Ariel Sharon to the Prime Minister's chair in 2001. Sharon, the champion of the Israeli right-wing camp, after the elections, turned against his traditional supporters. The new Prime Minister, dramatically, changed his strategy to cope with the situation in Gaza. Palestinian politics have been marred between democratic aspirations and the political agenda of radical Islamism. The "highlights" were undemocratic party wins in democratic elections (Hamas won a victory in Palestinian parliamentary elections in 2006[23]) and a bloody civil war in 2007 that "officially" divided Palestinian society.

Ariel Sharon, the primary architect of the settlement project, came to the conclusion that maintaining Israeli settlements in Gaza was costly, ineffective, and does not have any future. Under the impression that Israel does not have a "reliable Palestinian partner with which it can make progress in a two-sided peace process," Sharon led a dramatic unilateral move, known as "the Disengagement Plan." In 2005, the state of Israel evacuated "the Gaza Strip, including all existing Israeli towns and villages" (about 21 Jewish settlements) and dismantled four settlements in the Northern West Bank. The intention was to create a situation where there can "no longer be any permanent presence of Israeli security forces in the areas of Gaza Strip territory which have been evacuated" and in the areas of Northern West Bank that have been evacuated.[24] This historical and dramatic move was conducted without any negotiation, coordination, and cooperation with the Palestinians.

The Israeli unilateral withdrawal from the Gaza strip did not succeed in bringing peace and stability to the region, at least in the short run. Sadly it created momentum for new crises and complications. One of the major events following the Israeli unilateral disengagement was a coup d'état of Hamas in Gaza in 2007 that led to a split in Palestinian society.

Today, Palestinian society is geographically and politically divided. Gaza is controlled by the radical Islamist movement, Hamas. The West Bank is administered by the secular nationalist movement, PLO. Hamas in Gaza is committed to launching a holy war against Israel and establishing an Islamic autocracy in its place.[25] The PLO leadership in the West Bank is committed to finding a peaceful solution with Israel, based on the "two state solution,"[26] and gives the impression of serious intentions to form a democratic state.

The two entities, Gaza and the West Bank, began to develop different histories in their relationship with Israel. Gaza is under Israeli siege. The West Bank is under Israeli military occupation. The dominant motif in the relationship between the leadership of Israel and Hamas in Gaza is a violent dialogue that reached its peak in the Gaza war in 2008. The peace process between the leadership of Israel and the PLO in the West Bank is teetering between hope and despair.

Despite the difficult circumstances, the consensus solution to the conflict remained the "two state solution" – two independent states "Israel and Palestine, living side by side in peace and security." The questions are: Is the "two state solution" still a realistic option in the present tragic situation? How to promote peace and stability in the region? Is it not required to consider and develop a dual strategy to cope with the current complication (for example, one program to reduce the level of violence in the Israeli-Gaza crisis and the other to accelerate the train of peace in the Israeli-West Bank circumstances)?

The spectrum of possible solutions

What is the optimal solution to the Palestinian-Israeli conflict?

The mainstream discussion about the most advantageous solution to the Palestinian-Israeli conflict emerges between two extremes: "two state solution" on the one hand and "one state solution" on the other. The "two state solution" is the consensus solution while the "one state solution" did not get much support except maybe in marginal academic circles and some Palestinians in the Diaspora.[27] The framework of the "two state solution" is two separate independent states: a Jewish state (or, at least, a Jewish majority state) in Israel and a Palestinian state in Gaza and the West Bank. The principle of "one state solution" is one democratic state – including Israel, the West Bank, and Gaza – for the two people. The main motif of the "two state solution" is "divorce" (two separate independent states) while the central theme of the "one state solution" is a legal and political "marriage" between the two people under a democratic agreement that will guarantee citizenship and equal rights for all inhabitants.

My central claim is that the two competitive solutions, as attractive and appealing as they might sound to certain people, are not viable options. The two extreme alternatives, two states versus one state, can be very useful in helping us to sketch the spectrum of the discussion upon possible solutions to the Palestinian-Israeli conflict. However, again, the logic of the circumstances point to the fact that complete divorce ("two state solution") and legal marriage ("one state solution") are impossible to implement, at least in their extreme forms.[28]

The "divorce" solution – two separate states for the two people – is not a realistic option because the fate of the Palestinian and Israeli people is intertwined. It is close contact under high pressure that encompasses almost any aspect of social life, for example: *geographically* – there is no continuation of land between Gaza and the West Bank (the two parts of the Palestinian territories); *economically* – it is hard to imagine, at this stage at least, a Palestinian modern independent economy that provides a high rate of employment to the Palestinian people; *emotionally* – the two sides have strong ties to the old city of Jerusalem, an important place that, probably, will have to be monitored jointly under any kind of a peaceful solution; *politically* – a large portion of the Israeli citizens (about 25 percent) are relatives of the Palestinians in the territories (Arab-Israelis).

The marriage solution – one state for the two people – is also not a realistic proposal. The main reason is that the majority of Jewish Israelis, who are constantly afraid for their existence, are not willing even to consider it. For various reasons, most Jewish Israelis believe that the practical meaning of "one state solution" is the end of the only Jewish state in the world. If one of the parties – the intended groom or the future bride – does not want to get married than marriage is not an option, at least by peaceful means.

The extreme positions – marriage or divorce – are not viable options. The more realistic alternative is a combination of the extreme positions – an arrangement that proposes unity and diversity in one configuration. For example, any kind of arrangement that is based on two separate entities (the consensus solution) will have to include joint mechanisms to solve future disputes and coordinate cooperative activities. To put it differently, the two independent entities, Palestinian and Israeli, will have to be engaged in some kind of federal or confederal arrangement.[29]

Federation or confederation is not only a structure, it is also a process. In this book, I propose to look at it as a discovery process, a process where the two people discover how to establish a joint mechanism that can address a wide range of areas of joint needs. A major Palestinian-Israeli public negotiating congress – which is described and proposed in Chapter 7 (The public-assembly model) – can be the platform for establishing a joint mechanism for settling future disputes and coordinating joint activities. This peacemaking institution can turn into a peacekeeping institution once an effective peace agreement has been achieved. Of course, its main characteristics – such as structure, function, and authority – have to be discussed, negotiated, and decided by the two sides.[30]

Unfortunately, at this stage the two societies are far from reaching this point. A major obstacle is the political division in Palestinian society between Gaza, which is controlled by the radical Islamist movement Hamas, and the West Bank, which is administrated by the secular nationalist movement PLO. Despite the difficult circumstances, the consensus among analysts remains that the "two state solution" is the optimal resolution to the conflict. However, the conventional wisdom among many Israeli scholars is that the sad reality is no solution at all in the near future. The result is a paradigm shift in the strategy to cope with the Palestinian-Israeli struggle: from conflict-resolution to conflict-management.

3   Between conflict-resolutio and conflict-management

Resolvable or irresolvable conflict

The Palestinian-Israeli peace process is teetering between hope and despair. Despite 30 years of direct and indirect negotiations the dispute is still considered to be one of the most entrenched conflicts in the world. The consensus among many analysts is that everything has been said and tried in this desperate situation.

The disappointing results of infinite negotiations have led more and more scholars to believe that the conflict cannot be resolved in the near future. The two societies are simply not prepared to engage in an effective peace process that can lead the two people to accept a reasonable compromise. Replacing the violent struggle with a culture of peace takes time. It requires a paradigm shift in the strategy to cope with a struggle that might be irresolvable. Analysts have begun to focus upon developing techniques to manage the conflict instead of investing futile efforts in suggesting creative strategies to resolve it.

In general, we can identify two competitive trends in the extensive literature on peacemaking in the Palestinian-Israeli context: the conflict-management approach and the conflict-resolution strategy. The architects of the conflict-management strategy believe that the conflict cannot be resolved in the near future. They provide policy recommendations for improving the domestic and foreign position of each society in order to reduce the intensity of the irresolvable struggle. Hopefully, conditions for negotiation of a peace agreement will ripen in the future.[1] In contrast, the supporters of the conflict-resolution approach argue for returning to the negotiating table to achieve a final peace agreement as soon as possible and by any means.

It is quite acceptable to believe that the center of attention, especially among Israeli analysts, shifted from conflict-resolution to conflict-management after the failure of the Camp David summit in July 2000.[2] The Israeli mainstream narrative points out that Israeli Prime Minister Ehud

...arak offered Palestinian leader Yasser Arafat more than any other Israeli leader before him. Of particular significance was Barak's offer to work with Palestinian leaders in establishing an independent Palestinian state in the disputed territories including certain parts of East Jerusalem. According to the Israeli narrative, the Palestinians, or more precisely Yasser Arafat, refused to accept Barak's generous offer and decided to renew the violent struggle (the Second *Intifada*). Needless to say, Palestinians claim that the Israeli narrative is partial, biased, and an unfair description of the course of events.

In general, the Israeli conflict-management camp emphasizes that the struggle is asymmetrical. The meaning is that Israel is a modern state with functioning institutions, while the Palestinians, who lack the tradition of liberty, independence, and responsibility, have hardly made their first steps toward establishing a well functioning state.[3] A negotiation process at this stage is only going to bring violence, frustration, and despair. Moreover, the Israeli supporters of this strategy believe that any concessions to the Palestinians, who are not ready for a serious peace process, endanger the very existence of Israel. For example, Ariel Sharon's unilateral withdrawal from Gaza in 2005, which had given hope to most of the Israeli population, eventually brought only frustration and despair. Sharon's dramatic initiative was followed by a civil war among the Palestinians, a coup d'état of the militant Islamic movement Hamas in Gaza, and a severe escalation in the conflict between Israel and the Palestinians in Gaza.

The supporters of the conflict-resolution approach do not stand astonished, defeated and without reply. The conflict-resolution camp contends that trying to manage the conflict, reduce the level of violence, and improve the socio-political conditions within each society are certainly not enough to build the foundations for a peaceful social order. The lack of extensive negotiations is deepening the frustration in each society and strengthening the conviction that it is impossible to resolve the conflict by peaceful means. Each side continues to believe that there are no partners for peace on the other side (a phenomenon known as the mirrorimage[4]).

The combination of mutual suspicion and lack of serious negotiation, argue the conflict-resolution camp, is an ideal environment for extremists, radicals, and professional spoilers to dictate conditions for the rest of the people. For example, many Palestinians, who strive to live in their own independent state, continue to believe that the only language that Israelis understand is force. As a result, the radical Islamic movement, Hamas, gains more and more popularity in the streets of the West Bank and Gaza. In reaction many Israelis, who fear the rise of Palestinian religious fanaticism, give their votes to right-wing radicals "who know how to handle the situation."[5] In short, the unintended consequence of the conflict-management strategy is the deterioration of the relationships between the two sides and further escalation of the conflict.

It is hard to decide which approach – conflict-management or conflict-resolution – is the best strategy to bring peace and stability to the area. One of the main reasons is that there is an amount of truth in each position. Unfortunately, the two sides are entrenched in a bitter academic argument and often enough ignore each other's analysis, evaluation, and recommendations.

This bitter academic dispute, conflict-management versus conflict-resolution, is not new. It is a new version of an older academic argument. In the mid-1960s the Interactive Conflict Resolution paradigm challenged the traditional realist approach which had for decades dominated Peace and Conflict Resolution studies in International Relations. Ironically, given the subject matter, peace scholars became engaged in an intractable academic dispute. This academic struggle did not help them to develop a fresh, comprehensive paradigm that incorporates insights from the two competitive approaches in an integrated fashion. Rather, each camp has become more and more entrenched in its position and less convinced of the feasibility of the competing approach.

The historical debate

Peace research is a quite a new discipline in the academic world. It is hard to point out when exactly the study began to develop as an independent discipline.[6] However, it looks as if the formative years of this emerging academic profession began about 40 years ago when John Burton, one of the pioneers of peace research, began to develop his new pluralistic approach to the study of International Relations – "the World society paradigm."[7]

The dominant paradigm in International Relations in those days was classical realism. In general, key assumptions of realism are: states are dominant actors; force and power are their main instruments; and, security is a principal goal.[8] Realists believe that sovereign states, the key actors in international politics, are self-interested social entities which are constantly engaged in power contests.[9] The practical meaning is that keeping peace, order, and stability requires the application of questionable moral means which are associated with "power politics." Such tactics include sanctions, threats, and political manipulations.[10]

This paradigm gave some satisfactory answers to major security problems during the Cold War. During this era, the two superpowers competed to dictate and control the world order. One of the highlights of the realist paradigm was President Kennedy's peaceful resolution of the Cuban Missile Crisis, which threatened to destroy the world in 1962.[11]

Realists point out that their sophisticated doctrine provides a good explanation for one of the most astonishing miracles of the twentieth century – "50 years without a nuclear war."[12] A strategy that focuses on indirect communication and nuclear deterrence – "I know that you know that I know" – kept the two superpowers from destroying the world. However, we live in a complicated, dynamic, and ever changing world which faces infinite social problems. The realist paradigm did not succeed in providing satisfactory strategies to cope with many other social problems, distresses and crises, such as protracted intra-state conflicts. This is the place where the new pluralistic, "World Society paradigm," entered the picture.

The World Society paradigm presents a world perception that can be viewed as anti-realist. Its key assumptions contradict cornerstones in the traditional realist paradigm. According to the World Society paradigm, significant players in world politics are not only states but also include social groups such as political parties, ethnic communities, business firms, and social movements.[13] Their main goal is not only security but also satisfying human basic needs such as security, distinct identity, dignity, social justice, welfare and independence.[14] The most effective way to satisfy basic needs is cooperation through discussion, joint research, and cooperative exploration rather than the application of power, force, and deterrence.[15]

The new pluralist paradigm in International Relations has influenced the study of protracted social conflicts and their resolution.[16] The pluralistic approach emphasized that violent struggle is a poor strategy to achieve satisfaction of basic needs and fundamental human concerns. This fresh perspective has led to the development of a new discipline – Conflict Analysis and Resolution.[17] The analysis focuses upon discovering basic needs, concerns, and fears that led different groups to be engaged in intractable conflict. The resolution is an agreement that can satisfy those basic needs and give guarantees that can help the opposing factions to overcome their fears.[18] The peacemaking process becomes a problem that has to be solved by the opposing parties with the help of an impartial mediator that is not involved, at least not directly, in the struggle – a third party.

The first attempt to apply the new methodology, which Burton named "control communication," was a remarkable success. The case was a conflict that gathered momentum in Southeast Asia and involved Malaysia, Indonesia, and Singapore in the early 1960s. Burton organized a five-day workshop in London and invited representatives of the opposing governments and a panel of social experts to participate. The official purpose was an academic analysis and exploration of the roots of the struggle and not mediation for resolution and reconciliation.[19] After a careful analysis of the conflict the delegations and the panelists succeeded in sketching general guidelines and principles for resolution and settlement. The workshop led to a series of unofficial meetings in different forums, reestablishment of diplomatic contacts between the opposing governments, official negotiations, and a peace agreement in 1966.[20]

As Ronald Fisher notes, it is hard to quantify and measure the direct influence of the London workshop on the resolution of the Malaysia-Indonesia struggle. There are many other factors and elements that played an important role in the peacemaking process. However, it is clear that successive attempts to resolve destructive social conflicts by the application of unconventional methods of diplomacy developed by Burton and his followers did not appear to be as successful as the first experiment.[21] Perhaps the biggest failures of all are the infinite attempts to resolve the Palestinian-Israeli struggle by different methods of diplomacy, various techniques of conflict resolution, and involvement of several third-party mediators. The peacemaking methods of Burton and his followers that have been applied in the Middle East did not succeed in resolving the Palestinian-Israeli conflict.

Thirty years of ongoing efforts to resolve the Palestinian-Israeli conflict is a short time compared to the duration of "classical" intractable conflicts that tend to last for multiple decades. However, 30 years of peacemaking efforts is a very long time for people who live in the reality of an ongoing violent struggle. Should we not criticize, reexamine, and improve our peacemaking theories, approaches, and strategies?

Competition versus problem solving

The two competitive approaches, realism and pluralism, provide different tools to analyze and evaluate tragic situations of intractable conflicts. Realists interpret a conflict situation in terms of a power struggle between competing interests. Pluralists point out that fear and human needs are dominant motivations in protracted violent conflicts. Naturally, the different explanations of the dominant sources of conflicts led to diverse approaches to peacemaking.

Realists view peacemaking as an attempt to transform a destructive competition – the violent struggle – into a constructive contest which means negotiation by peaceful means. Pluralists envision peacemaking as an attempt to bring representatives of conflicting parties to a joint research of and exploration for "an agreement that addresses the fundamental needs and fears of both parties on a basis of reciprocity."[22]

Negotiation plays a key role in the two paradigms. But each approach emphasizes and concentrates on different aspects of the process. Realists emphasize the competitive aspects of negotiation – negotiation as bargaining. Pluralists view negotiation as a joint effort to find solutions to fundamental problems that are located in the center of the conflict – negotiation as a problem-solving process.[23] Let me demonstrate certain aspects of the controversy by looking at one of the most difficult obstacles for peace in the Palestinian-Israeli struggle – the city of Jerusalem.

From a realist perspective (bargaining position) both parties wish to have control over the city, or at least major parts of it. Therefore, any solution to the problem requires concessions and compromises. However, analyzing and understanding the dispute in terms of needs, concerns, and fears (a pluralistic perception) does not necessarily require compromises. For example, satisfaction of strong religious beliefs is not necessarily synonymous to ownership of the city. A peace agreement that allowed each side to visit the holy sites and worship its own god, under one arrangement or another, can satisfy religious needs. Pluralists argue that the opposing factions have to join forces in order to find an appropriate solution that can satisfy their basic needs on a basis of reciprocity. Needless to say, realists believe that a cooperative vision of peace making (the pluralistic approach), especially in the context of very difficult and sensitive issues, such as Jerusalem, is no more than an unrealistic utopia.

The dispute over the adequate terminology of negotiation (bargaining versus problem solving) reflects diverse viewpoints, different negotiation tactics, and semantic disagreements. It is beyond controversy that an ideal goal is to achieve a peace agreement that improves the positions of each side, satisfies basic needs, and resolves fundamental problems. However, realists argue that in the current situation it is almost impossible to get even close to the ideal. A main reason is that the Palestinians hardly made their first moves toward the establishment of a modern independent state. And states are the key actors in the realist paradigm. According to realism, it is impossible to achieve security and stability without the institutional framework of well-established states. At least until a Palestinian state has been established and begins to function diplomatically the conflict cannot be resolved and has to be managed.

The Israeli advocates of the conflict-management strategy – the new version of the realist paradigm – contend that any concessions to a state that does not exist (a failed Palestinian entity[24]) only endangers the very existence of the state of Israel. The Palestinians have not begun to establish a unified governmental system that can maintain law and order, is able to represent the interests of its people, and is capable of coping with strategic and existential problems. In this chaotic situation the Palestinians can be united only by a strong desire for the destruction of the state of Israel.[25] Analysts from the conflict-management camp provide policy recommendations to improve Israel's domestic and foreign position in a situation of irresolvable conflict. Hopefully, it will help to build the conditions for an effective future peace process.

The advocates of the conflict-resolution approach – the new version of the pluralist paradigm – point out that it will be impossible to manage the conflict (reducing the level of violence) without direct negotiations, at least in the long run. The Palestinian society, like the Israeli one, is built from different groups who have various concerns, needs, and interests. The only way to cope with the struggle is to find creative ways to satisfy basic needs of the different social entities through ongoing negotiations, discussions, and joint explorations. The lack of negotiation creates frustration and despair that are extremely costly for both sides. It gives the power to extremists, radicals, and spoilers – who are not interested in finding a reasonable solution to the struggle – and enables them to dictate the political agenda.

Like in the early days, advocates of the two camps are entrenched in a bitter intellectual battle. In the 1960s and 1970s the dispute in London was between the dominant realist paradigm (states are the primary actors who can bring collective security through the use of military and economic power) and the new, pluralistic, "world society" approach (cooperation between different social groups, who struggle to satisfy basic human needs, is necessary to resolve conflicts).[26] The tension and hostility rose to such a level that scholars of the two camps began failing each other's students.[27] In the present day, the old, bitter dispute appears under a different guise. Advocates of each camp – conflict-management (realism) and conflict-resolution (pluralism) – argue that the other's strategy is a proven recipe for a colossal disaster.

No doubt there is an amount of truth in the two competitive approaches. To put it differently, it is impossible to resolve the conflict without managing it, and vice versa. It is impossible to manage the conflict and reduce the level of intensified struggle without serious attempts to resolve it through negotiation, dialogue, and discussion that can give hope to the people. I suggest looking at the two competitive approaches, conflict-management versus conflict-resolution, as complementary: conflict-management and conflict-resolution.

In this book conflict-management and conflict-resolution are regarded as much broader concepts than their traditional forms. Conflict-management is a set of strategies which are designed to build the framework of a new peaceful social order. Conflict-resolution is a set of strategies which are built to shape the relationships between opposing societies through negotiations on multiple levels.

My central argument is that a multifaceted approach that implements insights from both the conflict-management and conflict-resolution approaches, in a unified form, has the greatest potential to build the foundations of a new peaceful social order in the Palestinian-Israeli case.

Part II

Interactive models of peacemaking

The second part of the book introduces four interactive models of peace-making. The first, *the strong-leader model*, involves dramatic unilateral initiatives taken by a strong leader of one of the parties. The second, *the social-reformer model*, encourages domestic reforms within each of the opposing societies. The third, *the political-elite model*, uses various forms of peacemaking interaction between political elites, as has been the dominant experience in the Palestinian-Israeli peace process. The fourth, *the public-assembly model*, proposes the creation of a major Palestinian-Israeli public negotiating congress, based loosely on the multi-party talks that helped to create a revolutionary change in South Africa and Northern Ireland.

The first two models, the strong-leader and the social-reformer, are con-flict-management models that define the boundaries of the peacemaking discussion. They are designed to shape the geopolitical structure of the conflict from different directions. The strong-leader type, characterized by unilateral moves by one of the parties, is a top-down model. The social-reformer type that consists of domestic reforms within each society is a bottom-up model. The strong-leader tries to create a situation that will lead to a solution that he or she favors (top-down). The social-reformer encourages domestic reforms within each of the opposing societies that can lead to peaceful relationships between them (bottom-up).

The third and fourth models, the political-elites and the public-assembly, are conflict-resolution models that are located between the extremes suggested by the strong leader and social reformer models. They are designed to shape the relationships between the two societies through direct interactions and negotiations on multiple levels. The political-elite model, characterized by various forms of interactions between political elites from both sides, is a top-down model. The public-assembly model, exemplified by the proposal to establish a major Palestinian-Israeli public negotiating congress, intends to create peacemaking pressure from the bottom-up.

Let me briefly elaborate on these four models:

- *The strong-leader model* calls for a sophisticated, effective, and efficient leader to shape the framework of the conflict by unilateral political, diplomatic, or militaristic moves. Classical examples are: Anwar Sadat's astonishing peacemaking visit in 1977 to the Israeli parliament in Jerusalem; Ariel Sharon's unilateral withdrawal from Gaza in 2005; and the release in 1990 of Nelson Mandela from prison by the last president of apartheid South Africa, Frederik Willem de Klerk.
- *The social-reformer model* recommends building the foundations of a peaceful social order by first encouraging Israelis and Palestinians to improve the socio-political conditions in their respective societies. Building the foundations of a good, decent, and stable social order in Israel and the Palestinian territories are critical preconditions for beginning an effective peacemaking process. Moreover, it helps to ensure that if the peace process collapses the results are not going to be as disastrous as they have been in the past.
- *The political-elite model* offers various diplomatic channels. These forms of interaction can serve as effective tools for policy makers and political elites who are determined to begin a peace process, support it, and finalize agreements. An archetypical example is the Oslo peace process of the 1990s.
- *The public-assembly model* offers a mechanism (a public negotiating congress) to involve the people from both sides in the peacemaking process. The main function of the negotiations in the congress is to provoke a public debate within each society, to influence people's opinion, to invite an effective peacemaking force to the stage of politics, and to press the opposing leadership to reach agreements.

Table 1 presents the four models according to different categories:

The classification choice of conflict-management or conflict-resolution is dependent on the presence of negotiations as a central feature in each one of these models. The strong-leader and the social-reformer (the conflict-management models) may suggest opening moves toward negotiations but they do not provide frameworks for the actual negotiations. In contrast, the

Table 1

Direction	Category	Conflict-management	Conflict-resolution
Top-down		Strong-leader	Political-elite
Bottom-up		Social-reformer	Public-assembly

political-elite and the public-assembly (the conflict-resolution models) suggest various forms of negotiations at different levels.

Each one of these models offers critical insights for the peacemaking efforts in the Middle East. However, none of them can create the conditions for an effective peace process by itself. The challenge of peacemaking is to create a multifaceted peacemaking strategy that integrates insights from these four models in an integrated fashion. This is the main argument of this book.

4   The strong-leader model

Introduction

The "strong-leader" model entails a unilateral action by one of the parties
to shift the geopolitical framework of the conflict. In general this action is
taken by a strong leader whose domestic political control enables him or her
to take steps that have the form of concessions on the other side. The unilateral initiative might be political, diplomatic or military in nature. What is
crucial is that the strong leader attempts to promote some kind of solution,
or more precisely his or her favorable solution, to the conflict in the event of
a stalled peace process.

Political leaders, who tried to create a momentum for conflict resolution by
making drastic moves, changed the frameworks of the Arab-Israeli struggle
and the Palestinian-Israeli conflict. The first was Egyptian President Anwar
Sadat, whose astonishing arrival in Israel in 1977 paved the way to a peace
agreement between the two nations. The second is Israeli Prime Minister
Ariel Sharon, who led a unilateral and historic withdrawal from Gaza and
areas of the northern West Bank in 2005. The conventional wisdom is that
the first was a success while the second led to disaster.

This chapter constructs and presents the "strong-leader" model, evaluates
its implications and explains the lessons it provides for peacemaking initiatives. Let us begin by providing a theoretical background and formulating
basic assumptions.

The road to hell is paved with good intentions

The "strong-leader" model is based on the idea that any solution to civil
strife and intractable conflict depends on the unusual and dramatic initiatives of strong political leaders. This idea is rooted in a long tradition of
political thought beginning with a short treatise, *The Prince*, written 500
years ago by Niccolo Machiavelli.

The Prince is a unique exploration of the mystery of politics. It is composed as an advice book for the common authoritarian leader who has an unlimited appetite for political power. Machiavelli's horrible and shocking advice gives the impression that the study of leadership and statecraft is an advanced course in the academy of crime. Therefore, at least at first blush, it is very difficult to imagine that Machiavelli offers any insights that could be useful in peacemaking. After all, the standard methods of peacemaking are finding ways to build trust and a basis for cooperation, not trickery, crime, or indecent manipulation. Nevertheless, it is important to remember the historical context of Machiavelli's writings – a time of endless civil wars and intractable conflict.

Machiavelli's time is well remembered as a period of social collapse. It was a tragic age of endless wars and civil strife rendering Italy into violent regional rivalry. However, in contrast to the destructive reality, the conventional wisdom was that any decent society should be directed according to moral ideals rooted in tradition such as those of the church and moral philosophy. The general idea, which sounds simple and attractive, was that only a moral society has the potential to diminish evils, wrongs, and destruction. Accordingly, professional politics and statecraft were understood as an ethical mission for well-educated intellectuals with special expertise in ethics and morality.[1] It was a utopian vision of politics, which blocked any possibility of developing a political strategy to lead society to overcome continuous bloody conflicts. In writing *The Prince*, Machiavelli turned conventional wisdom on its head.[2]

It seems that Machiavelli understood very well – and sometimes too well – that the road to hell is paved with moral ideals and good intentions. To shake the very foundations of this utopian vision, he called Satan to the Italian crown. Machiavelli's prime candidate to lead the Italian people to national salvation is a sophisticated brutal gangster. The inevitable question is: Is it not too much of an exaggeration to raise the idea of a criminal leading society in a difficult situation of social crisis?

To understand the logic behind Machiavelli's seemingly grotesque proposal and the lessons it offers for intractable conflicts, we must remember that *The Prince* is only one of Machiavelli's great political treatises.

The Machiavellian transformation

Niccolo Machiavelli's most famous political treatises are two compositions that seem to be, at first blush at least, in direct contradiction: *The Prince* and *The Discourses*. *The Prince* is composed in the manner of a handbook for the common authoritarian leader, while *The Discourses* is an exceptional republican treatise. Ironically, in the dedication of each of these books, Machiavelli claims he is presenting everything he knows. Therefore, one might wonder: Who was the real Machiavelli – a champion of authoritarianism or a passionate advocate of republicanism?[3]

It looks like part of this mystery can be resolved in the last chapter of *The Prince*. In this section Machiavelli opens his heart and reveals his prime political dream – the unification of Italy and the restoration of glory to Rome. In the final chapter it becomes clear that Machiavelli tried to motivate and even manipulate a hungry leader to develop the political power necessary to unite Italy and restore glory to ancient Rome.[4] Under the assumption that Machiavelli did not suffer from split personality, the last chapter makes it possible to see *The Discourses* as the natural continuation of *The Prince*.

The Prince is stage one – stopping the civil wars and uniting Italy, while *The Discourses* is stage two – preventing the new social order from sliding back into chaos by building the foundations for a stable republic.[5] *The Prince* presents a desperate solution to intractable conflict and civil wars while *The Discourse* provides the recipe to build and preserve a decent, stable, republic. The glue which connects these two stages is a criminal authoritarian leader (*The Prince*) who miraculously transforms into a benevolent dictator who wins his place forever in history as the founder of a decent, stable, republic (*The Discourses*). The leader who begins in infamy ends in virtue.

It is of little surprise that a dramatic Machiavellian shift can be found in the biography of the two heroes of this chapter: Anwar Sadat and Ariel Sharon.

The Machiavellian tradition

The classical republican interpretation of *The Prince,* which I briefly sketched in the preceding section, may sound elegant and appealing. However, it is not clear at all whether it is true, half true, or completely false. Moreover, it gives Machiavelli a saintly image when it is not at all clear if he deserves it. However, whether the interpretation is true or false, *The Prince* remains notable in the pantheon of social ideas. Part of the reason is that *The Prince* is a sign post in the beginning of a long tradition of scholarship embracing the idea that a post-civil war peaceful social order can emerge only after a strong authoritarian transitional period.[6] This tradition, begun with Machiavelli and continued with Thomas Hobbes, also encompasses contemporary thinkers such as Samuel Huntington and protagonists of the free market system, such as Friedrich A. Hayek.[7]

Paradoxically, these scholars, who are well known as advocates of personal liberty, believe that the only solution to difficult civil wars and intractable conflicts is a state builder-dictator. The idea is that the transformation of social chaos to a decent social order can only emerge after a transitional authoritarian period in which the institutional and constitutional foundations for stability are established.[8] Friedrich Hayek, a passionate advocate of the free market system as the only feasible alternative to tyranny and fascism, formulated it forcefully:

> "When a government is in a situation of rupture, and there are no recognized rules . . . it is practically inevitable for someone to have almost absolute powers . . . It may seem a contradiction that it is I of all people who am saying this, I who plead for limiting government's powers in people's lives and maintain that many of our problems are due, precisely, to too much government. However, when I refer to this dictatorial power, I am talking of a transitional period, solely. As a means of establishing a stable democracy and liberty, clean of impurities. This is the only way I can justify it – and recommend it."[9]

There is no doubt that Machiavelli and Hayek use appealing rhetoric. In desperate situations it is attractive to aspire for the emergence of a strong peace-making leader. However, the basic questions that the Machiavellian tradition struggles to explain are: How can we guarantee that the strong leader is a benevolent dictator, who takes power to complete his historical peacemaking task? How could we be certain that the strong leader is a republican autocrat (Machiavelli) or a liberal dictator (Hayek)? Did Machiavelli and Hayek forget rulers, autocrats, and strong leaders who never intended to wear the royal clothes of the redeemer?

The solution, or at least part of the solution, to such difficult questions can be found in the pages of *The Prince*. Machiavelli, in his shocking yet brilliant rhetoric, offers a simple cost and benefit analysis. If an absolute ruler, cruel as he might be, does not act for the benefit of his society (at least in the final account), he will not long survive.[10] And acting for the benefit of society means quelling the civil wars, uniting Italy and restoring glory to Rome.

As attractive and brilliant as Machiavelli's insights may seem, we dare never shrink from questioning and wondering: Can a selfish ruler actually fulfill such a difficult mission? Should we trust a strong ruler to follow Machiavelli's way of thinking? Should we believe that dictators necessarily perceive an overlap between their survival and all crucial altruistic tasks for the benefit of their society, in any final account?

Reading *The Prince* with careful attention indicates that this puzzling composition actually emerges in some twilight zone between imagination and reality.[11] On the one hand, Machiavelli has constructed an imaginary figure of a legendary criminal dictator. On the other hand, it seems that our sophisticated author does not entirely trust "real" human autocrats to understand the pure logic of his super arch-criminal. In other words, there is a gap between Machiavelli's construction of the ideal gangster-ruler and his expectations that real life human princes will understand and follow his insights on the most efficient means of statecraft. In order to close the gap, Machiavelli promised his unreliable human prince a precious prize – world fame and a place in history forever – if he devotes himself to the restoration of order in the Italian society.[12] By appealing to the prince's narcissistic impulses, Machiavelli attempts to motivate him to undertake great and noble tasks for the benefit of his society.[13]

Unfortunately, most rulers do not read Machiavelli or Hayek. History demonstrates that dictators and rulers make for themselves, at their own whims, their own rules of conduct. And generally their behavior does not follow Machiavelli's logic in general nor his advice in particular. Nevertheless, the sad history of protracted conflicts in the Middle East seems to demonstrate many of the insights that Machiavelli offers in his political writings.

Between Machiavellian peacemakers and intractable conflict

Political leaders, who designed and initiated drastic moves in order to create a momentum for conflict resolution, changed the geopolitical structure of the Arab-Israeli struggle and the Palestinian-Israeli conflict. These leaders were certainly not saints and their political actions did not necessarily arise from noble intentions – to say the least. The first was Anwar Sadat, the President of Egypt, whose astonishing trip to Israel in 1977 paved the way for negotiation of a peace agreement between the two nations. The second is Ariel Sharon, the Israeli Prime Minister, who stood against his party and traditional right-wing supporters in leading a unilateral and historical withdrawal from Gaza and northern areas of the West Bank.[14] Ironically, Sadat, the Egyptian dictator, led the peace process through negotiation and cooperation while, Sharon, the democratically elected prime minister, conducted his dramatic move without any coordination, cooperation, and involvement of the Palestinians.

It may be difficult, if even impossible, to fathom the true motivations at work behind the behaviors and activities of human beings. We do not have X-rays into Sadat's and Sharon's minds and souls to explore directly their way of thinking. But combining the logic of the circumstances (or the complexity of the situation) with insights from Machiavelli's school for statecraft might help us construct a "good" story. And a "good" story, or a fable, whether it is true, half true, or completely imaginary, offers a lesson. Accordingly, I will sketch a Machiavellian interpretation of Sadat and Sharon's historic and dramatic moves.

Looking back at the disconsolate financial situation of Egypt, and the immense social problems resulting from there, indicates that Egypt desperately needed an "economic fuel".[15] It is quite reasonable to surmise that

Anwar Sadat, who challenged the very existence of Israel in the 1973 war, did not abandon his old desire to return the Sinai desert back to Egyptian control. This magical desert, one of the most beautiful places in the world, has economic, political, and strategic value: oil fields, potential to attract tourists from all over the world, and control over the Suez Canal. But it seems that the Egyptian leader felt trapped. On the one hand, it was quite clear to him from past painful experiences that it will be extremely difficult to recover the lost asset by force and violence. On the other hand, recovering the desert by peaceful means also appeared impossible. This is because the leadership of Israel, which lives in a continuous, profound state of concern for Israel's continued existence,[16] was engaged in an uncompromising foreign policy. Israel's policy compelled Sadat to understand that the routine and conventional means of diplomacy and negotiation were only doomed to failure.

Any attempt to build bridges between Egypt and Israel was inevitably received with extreme suspicion. Even the most optimistic statesmen were skeptical over the genuine intentions of the two bitter rivals to reach a peace agreement.[17] In defiance of any "rational" prediction, the Egyptian leader made an astonishing move – in 1977, Sadat, the leader of the strongest Arab country and most rigidly entrenched of Israel's enemies, came to Jerusalem to talk peace in the Israeli parliament, the Knesset. Unsurprisingly, this visit was a turning point in the Arab-Israeli conflict.

However, it is not completely fanciful to consider that this dramatic turning point was part of a manipulative strategy by the Egyptian leader, intent on reclaiming the Sinai desert through a peace agreement with Israel and establishing strong relationships with the United States.[18] Indeed, following the peace treaty of 1979: Israel was to turn over to Egypt the Sinai desert – including oil fields and Israeli air bases (for civilian purposes). In addition, Egypt was to receive massive economic and military aid from the United States – two billion dollars in military equipment and foreign aid of one billion dollars.[19] Therefore, Sadat's historic move seems to rewrite one of the basic rules of *The Prince*: not every subversive manipulation is indecent, at least in the final account.[20] Nevertheless, Machiavelli's methods of diplomacy, often enough, demonstrate concretely that many peacemaking efforts look like the continuation of war by peaceful means.[21]

Ariel Sharon, the legendary warrior, has many dubious "credits" in the Palestinian-Israeli conflict. For example, it is hard to forget that in 1989, Sharon led aggressive political moves to prevent the Israeli government from negotiating and compromising with the Palestinians.[22] The same Ariel Sharon, who devoted a major part of his life to build, expand, and strengthen Jewish settlements in the disputed territories, led a historical "one-sided withdrawal" from Gaza and a small area in the West Bank. The "father" of the settlements came to the conclusion that the project does not have any future in the Gaza strip (for example, the high birth rate of Palestinians in Gaza made altering the demographic reality in favor of Israel a highly unlikely possibility). In order to create "a better security, political, economic and demographic situation" for Israel, it is better to leave Gaza forever. "In any future permanent status arrangement, there will be no Israeli towns and villages in the Gaza strip."[23] In the short run, the unilateral move convinced many Israelis that the occupation might be more harmful than beneficial to the existence of Israel. I would like to expand and explain.

It can scarcely escape notice how much of the Jewish experience is devastatingly tragic and traumatic: the historically fresh and fairly recent trauma of endless pogroms culminating in the Holocaust along with the ancient, ingrained, and painful memory of the destruction of the Second Temple around AD 70. Indeed, a common refrain in Jewish prayer is: "every generation they tried to exterminate us but we survived."[24] A society in which a major part of the culture and tradition is based on traumas naturally tends to be a fortified society and not an open one. In other words, people who are always worried in the back of their minds about their very survival will not readily compromise on issues concerning their security.[25] A noticeable "symptom" in the Jewish Israeli[26] experience has always been the absence of any serious public debate on fundamental issues relating to the existence of Israel, for example: What are the borders of the country? What is the fate of Jerusalem? Which concessions does Israel have to make in order to promote peace and stability in the region?

The evacuation of the Gaza strip and a small area in the West Bank, which entailed evacuating Jewish people from their homes against their will, was not an easy experience for Jewish Israelis. It recalls black spots in Jewish history, in which Jewish people were forced to wander from place to place. Ariel Sharon's style of leadership enabled him to bypass major domestic and international barriers and made the initiative extremely dramatic. On the one hand, Sharon established a broad coalition and succeeded to play the system. He led the initiative despite the objection of major forces within his party and against massive opposition from his traditional right-wing supporters. On the other hand, Sharon, an archetypical example of a strong leader, conducted the Israeli withdrawal without any agreement with the Palestinians and without receiving anything in exchange.

In spite of major concerns in the Israeli public, the unilateral withdrawal was carried off smoothly, efficiently, and peacefully, despite isolated incidents. The event did not endanger the very existence of the state, at least not in the short run. Accordingly, a major part of the Israeli population began to seriously consider the idea that even in times of intractable conflict, when a reasonable peace negotiation seems to be an unrealistic option, Israel is strong enough to lead one-sided initiatives. Moreover, a one-sided withdrawal might be more beneficial to the survival of Israel than a continued, unnecessary occupation. Unfortunately, the Israeli euphoria did not last long. There are pivotal players in the political and militaristic game that do not follow Israeli peacemakers' hopes, wishes, and expectations.

The unilateral disengagement signaled to the Palestinians that they have to begin serious efforts to establish an independent state, at least in the Gaza strip. And independence and freedom mean responsibility. The burden of responsibility requires establishing institutions, dismantling paramilitary groups, fighting corruption, providing decent education and all the basic provisions that any modern, desirable society must devote itself to in perpetuity. However, the Palestinian people do not necessarily speak in one voice. Terms such as freedom, responsibility, and a decent society, have different meanings to different political parties. As soon as the withdrawal began, a violent power struggle began to erupt within Palestinian society. The violence occurred both within the ranks of the secular, nationalistic PLO and between the PLO and the Islamist militant movements Hamas and Islamic Jihad. The climax of the struggle for control of the Gaza strip was a civil war between the Fatah, the largest faction of the PLO, and Hamas in 2007, about two years after the disengagement. The civil war ended with Hamas, one of Israel's most entrenched enemies, taking control over Gaza in 2007.[27]

If there is any truth in my interpretation of Sadat's and Sharon's ways of thinking then it is worth recalling and reexamining Machiavelli's brilliant insight into how the personal ambitions of a "hungry" leader are supposed to operate for the benefit of society. In Sadat's case, Egypt acquired Sinai and both countries gained peace. However, in Sharon's situation, the unilateral withdrawal so far has not created a momentum for peacemaking, to say the very least. The collapse of the Palestinian authority and the political split between Gaza and the West Bank has turned the Palestinian-Israeli struggle into a triangle of very problematic relationships: Israel and Hamas in Gaza; Israel and the PLO in the West Bank; PLO in the West Bank and Hamas in Gaza (which has direct influence upon the Palestinian-Israeli struggle and possibilities for its resolution).

Despite the tragic situation, it is reasonable to assume that Sharon's personal ambitions to stay in power and retain his tenure, and not to lose the Prime Minister's chair as did his predecessors, Benjamin Netanyahu and Ehud Barak, motivated him to lead such a drastic move. It seems that Sharon understood that holding the bridle of power depended upon the ability to act for the benefit of society. And the benefit of society depends, first and foremost, on the ability to progress to some kind of resolution of a difficult, intractable conflict.[28] However, the salient question remains: Should we simply wait until a "hungry" leader at long last discovers an overlap between his personal narcissistic ambitions to stay in power and the possibility of breaking the deadlock of intractable conflict by a unilateral drastic move?

The strong-leader model – risks and evaluation

As attractive and heroic as our two short stories of dramatic initiatives might sound, the final results, so far, are not as glorious as in fairytales. The relationship between Egypt and Israel has never evolved beyond a cold peace and the Palestinian-Israeli relationship has teetered between a few moments of hope in the West Bank-Israeli situation and complete despair in the Gaza-Israeli case. The inevitable conclusion is that dramatic initiatives of strong political leaders are not enough to build and maintain a beneficial, peaceful, social order.

The political situations of Egypt, Israel, and the Palestinians lack the necessary social foundations to establish a fruitful and peaceful relationship. However, there is a big difference between cold peace (Egypt–Israel), stalled peace process (West Bank–Israel), and destructive violent struggle (Gaza–Israel). It might be that in the current situation, cold peace is the best that can be achieved between Egypt and Israel. However, the Palestinians and the Israelis cannot afford to continue their protracted, violent struggle.

Egypt and Israel are two functioning states with stable regimes and established institutions. It has been relatively easy for both sets of authorities to keep agreements and maintain a cold peace. In contrast, the Palestinian people have hardly made their first steps toward independence. The Palestinian authority faced major domestic socio-political problems that characterize modernizing entities in transition, such as dysfunction of the political system and major difficulties in maintaining law and order.[29] It should be a matter of little surprise to students of social affairs that the events following Sharon's unilateral withdrawal were the collapse of the Palestinian Authority, which then complicated the situation beyond any imagination.

Machiavellian peacemakers are not superhuman. They can try to begin a peace process in a stalled situation. Their dramatic actions sometimes break entrenched conventions. Their actions might even create momentum for negotiations. But they cannot create a peaceful social order by drastic unilateral moves without the existence of basic socio-political foundations. Moreover, unilateral dramatic actions can create political and social chain reactions that cannot be fully anticipated and controlled. The existence of effective socio-political mechanisms that can maintain and provide political order can help ensure that societies in conflict zones will survive the shock of unilateral drastic actions and will not collapse into chaos.

Sharon penetrated into the Israeli mindset the belief that the occupation is more harmful than beneficial. His disengagement put the end to the utopian dream of "Greater Israel" and suggested that a beneficial peace will require major concessions from the Israelis. Despite the fact that a major part of Sharon's party and many of his right-wing former allies opposed the disengagement, the majority of the population in Israel enthusiastically supported the unilateral withdrawal. For the majority of Israelis, Sharon became once more the "King of Israel."

However, the "King" did not have the opportunity to observe the following crises: civil wars among the Palestinians, the collapse of the Palestinian authority, the continuing rocket attacks launched in Gaza against Israeli cities, and the Gaza war during the winter of 2008–09. On January 4, 2006, a short period of time after the disengagement, Sharon became severely ill and needed to step out of politics and public life for good. A major part of the Israeli public still wonders: How would Sharon react to the new situation that his dramatic initiative was not intended to create? Did he have a backup plan? Did Sharon, the military tactician, prepare a strategy and political program to promote peace between Israel and the Palestinians in the West Bank?

Like many strong political leaders, Sharon did not share with the general public his future plans, if he had any. Among many Israelis the myth of Ariel Sharon as a warrior, general, and political leader did not lose its appeal. There are Israelis, desperate from the difficult situation, who continue to believe that Ariel Sharon would have known how to handle the situation better than anyone else.[30]

One of the immediate consequences of the peace process between Egypt and Israel was that no Arab state would try to go to war with Israel. This achievement has contributed to the Palestinization of the Arab-Israeli conflict (the disengagement of Arab states from the conflict and leaving it to the Palestinians)[31] and to the breaking of former Egyptian president and Sadat predecessor Gamal Abdel Nasser's utopian dream about pan-Arabism (two tendencies that actually started after the Six-Day War). On the other hand, Sadat's initiative added to the vacuum in the Arab world, which was created after the failure of the pan-Arabism aspirations, and enabled the rise of political Islam. Unfortunately, Sadat paid a dear price for his peace initiative – on October 6, 1981, he was assassinated by a radical Islamist.

The strong-leader model – conclusion and recommendations

The strong leader model requires unilateral action by one of the parties to shift the geopolitical framework of a conflict. It must be carried out by a powerful political leader who promotes some kind of solution to the struggle during a stalled peace process. It is a top-down conflict-management strategy; the unilateral move is not intended to solve the conflict but rather to create conditions that favor the strong leader's vision of peacemaking. Indeed, after Sadat's diplomatic offensive, the two parties were still far away from reaching an agreement. A long frustrating negotiating process, under the mediation of former US President Jimmy Carter, was required to find compromises that would breach the gaps.[32]

The strong leader could be a dictator like Sadat or a democratically elected prime minister like Sharon. What is important is that the leader's domestic political control enables him or her to carry out a dramatic initiative that could have a drastic impact on the political situation. The initiative could be characterized as diplomatic (Sadat), military (Sharon), or political.[33]

The major weakness of the strong-leader model is its dependency upon the drastic maneuvers of political rulers. Political leaders, especially ambitious political leaders, should not always be trusted. Their actions could be very dangerous and might cause more harm than benefit. As the conflicts in the Middle East demonstrate, to wait until a strong political leader like Sadat or Sharon emerges on the political stage is a very costly and risky strategy.

The second weakness is that unilateral initiatives, as dramatic and sophisticated as they may be, usually are not enough to build a beneficial, peaceful, social order. These kinds of moves might bring beneficial results, such as the beginning of a fruitful peace process, only in an appropriate socio-political structure that can help the societies to survive the shock (a lesson from the comparison between the cases of Sadat and Sharon). However, it is important to remember that the strong-leader model is a desperate strategy. In a situation of endless violent struggle, unilateral dramatic actions might be the only option to progress some kind of solution to the conflict. Indeed, the strong-leader model, in situations of social collapse, is advocated by champions of freedom and independence (for example, Friedrich Hayek).

Sometimes it looks like the unilateral action, carried out by a strong influential political leader, is the only way to break old taboos and entrenched conventions that prevent any peaceful discussion between rival societies. For example, Sadat's initiative broke the longstanding Israeli perception that it is impossible to make peace with Arabs. Sharon's unilateral withdrawal demonstrated for many Israelis the idea that the occupation could be more damaging than beneficial.

The strong leader, who intends to lead a unilateral initiative, has to remember that he or she is not alone in the political game (many strong leaders tend to forget this). The ruler has to bear in mind that leadership carries a lot of responsibility. Accordingly, the strong leader must ask himself some of the following questions before carrying out any drastic measure:

- Are unilateral actions my last resort?
- What are the potential negative consequences of unilateral actions?

- Under what conditions is the other side most likely to cooperate?
- How can dramatic, unilateral actions promote future negotiations?
- Are the opposing societies prepared to respond effectively to the consequences of unilateral moves?
- Is there an international backup in case of disaster?

In conclusion, the "strong-leader model", or unilateral moves by one side of a conflict, cannot sustain a peace process by itself. When there are no other options, the unilateral action has to be carried out, but it must be combined with important elements that the other models suggest.

5   The social-reformer model

Introduction

The social-reformer agrees with the strong-leader that the conflict cannot be resolved in the near future by conventional methods of peacemaking and conflict resolution. He reminds us that most of the infinite attempts to negotiate solutions by political-elites of the opposing societies have ended, so far, with frustration, despair and, even, disaster. There is an urgent need for a different kind of thinking to cope with this miserable situation.

The social-reformer is also very critical of the desperate strategy that the strong-leader proposes. He is afraid that unilateral dramatic moves that are carried out by a strong political leader, who is determined to shape the geopolitical structure of the conflict, can cause more harm than good. Those unilateral moves are extremely dangerous in situations where the opposing societies lack the basic foundations of a new social order that the strong leader is motivated to construct. The collapse of the Palestinian Authority in 2007 after Sharon's unilateral moves demonstrates the danger of this situation.

The social-reformer focuses on creating opportunities for resolving the conflict by encouraging domestic reforms within the opposing societies. Like the strong-leader model, the social-reformer model is aimed at managing the conflict within some constructive bounds rather than resolving it outright. However, instead of calling on the authority of a strong leader to impose a unilateral dramatic move, it encourages each society to improve its position by focusing on domestic policy. To put it differently, the social-reformer model addresses the question: "How do we resolve the conflict?" by first asking, "How do we build the foundations of a good society in time of conflict?" If the strong-leader model aims to reshape the conflict from the top down, the social-reformer model means to do so from the bottom up.

The social-reformer model draws on the idea of constitutional economists, like James Buchanan, and political scientists, like Samuel Huntington, that an adequate framework of rules and institutions is a necessary condition for the transformation of social chaos to a peaceful social order.[1] In our context, domestic reforms that improve the internal cohesion of each society, the rule of law, and the accountability of political leaders may help the population in both societies to discover the value of peace and explore opportunities how to reach it. These necessary conditions have the potential to create the foundations for an effective peace process and reduce the impact of radicals, extremists, and "professional" spoilers.

Political-elites and social experts

In 2002, a group of Israelis and Palestinians elites gathered in Geneva in order to search for a comprehensive solution to their tragic struggle. The participants, who included political-elites and social experts, conducted a comprehensive study that provided solutions to the most difficult issues in one of the most complicated struggles in the world, the Palestinian-Israeli conflict.

No doubt the Geneva accord contributed to the growing consensus that the "two state solution" is the optimal solution to the conflict. Moreover, it is quite clear that anyone who wishes to explore possible solutions to the conflict will use, consider, and evaluate some of the thoughtful insights that this impressive study suggests.[2] However, this valuable accord, which looks so remarkable on paper, failed to bring salvation in reality.

The Geneva accord did not succeed in mobilizing the opposing societies in the direction of a two state solution. Moreover, after the Palestinian civil war in 2007, it is not clear if a two state solution is a viable option anymore. The Palestinian society is politically divided between Gaza and the West Bank. The leadership in each entity – Hamas (the radical Islamist movement) in Gaza and the PLO (the national secular party) in the West Bank – is committed to a different political agenda. The questions are: How can the opposing societies use and implement valuable insights from the Geneva accord to promote peace and stability in the region? What role should social experts and political-elites play in our struggle to cope with the most burning, difficult, and existential problems of the region? Is it possible to implement creative ideas that political-elites and social scientists, who have conducted a comprehensive study on the issues at stake, recommend to society in crisis?

The call for political elites and social experts to solve our misery and most difficult social problems was not invented in the Geneva accord. The role of specialists in bringing solutions to our problems and designing a better social order belongs to one of the most basic and fundamental problems in humanities and the social sciences: How to build the foundations of a good society?

The historical debate and the big experiment

How does one build and conduct a stable, peaceful, and decent social order?

History shows that the struggle toward building the foundations of a decent, stable social order is unending. The dynamics and complexity of our social life lead to infinite problems and various unexpected crises. Indeed, the enemy threatening the very existence of any human society is constantly changing its disguise. The diversity of opinions over the optimal way to build the foundations of a good society is, usually, shaped by the urgent problem at stake.

In the beginning of the twentieth century the most severe social problems were not intractable conflict and civil war but the rise and flourishing of totalitarian regimes. Toward the middle of the twentieth century the most critical problems were encompassed under the questions: How does society prevent the resurgence of tyranny and dictatorship? How to avoid the repetition of the same mistakes?

Around the end of the Second World War, the intellectual mainstream, including the likes of the well-known sociologist Karl Manheim, was searching for rational ways to prevent such social crises. The hard core of scholars, who overestimated human intellectual power, believed in the possibility of creating a better world by rational planning and marshalling of society. They were entrenched in the utopian belief that almost every social problem can be solved rationally by social experts. Social planners have to sketch a master plan in their "laboratory" for building the foundations of a decent stable society. "Modern Socialism," defined as rational planning of the foundations of a good society, became the ultimate alternative to Fascism.[3]

In our days, the conventional wisdom shifted. After the failure of the biggest experiment in centrally planned society – the collapse of the Soviet Union – it is clear that rational planning of society is an impossible mission for human beings. Social experts, like any human being, are limited in their ability to cope with the complexity of our social life. Social life does not provide the optimal conditions for social engineering, to say the very least. Every administrative, political, and militaristic move – dictated by leaders, policy makers, and experts – enfold unintended consequences that cannot be fully anticipated. The creation and rise of the Hamas movement, a militant outgrowth of the Muslim Brotherhood in the Palestinian territories, demonstrates that unintended consequences can sometimes cause problems and difficulties that are almost impossible to bypass, solve, and correct.

Until the 1980s, Israel did not move against the Muslim Brotherhood, while they had taken firm actions against its national secular rival, the PLO. The Muslim Brotherhood restricted itself to nonviolent and non-political actions (charity, education, and other social activities), while the PLO was considered to be a terrorist organization. The Israeli leadership saw the growing popularity of the Muslim Brotherhood, as a non-violent social force that could counteract the actions of the violent secular PLO. The creation of Hamas out of the Muslim Brotherhood in 1987 (the first *Intifada*) turned this optimistic convention on its head. Hamas was discovered as one of Israel's most entrenched and violent enemies.[4] The questions are: Is there a way to control unintended consequences? Is there a social mechanism that is able to navigate unintended consequences of political, social and militaristic actions for the benefit of society? What can be a viable alternative to rational methods in order to construct a better social order?

The new socialist paradigm, rational planning of society, is replaced with a liberal world view, which emphasizes the importance of creating the conditions that can lead to a constructive process. Peacemaking is not restricted to implementing specific solutions to the conflict but to creating the conditions where the opposing factions discover the road to peace and prosperity. Peacemaking becomes a discovery process.

Social competition is a central motif in the "new" liberal paradigm. Social competition is a broad concept that can be viewed as a process, structure and, even, metaphor.[5] In our context, the question is: How does one transform the violent struggle, which can be regarded as a destructive competition, into a constructive contest, which means negotiation by peaceful means?

Between constructive and destructive competition

Protagonists of the free market system envision an ideal structure of society as a multi dimensional competitive market. The ideal society is built from small competitive markets – such as ethics, politics, and the market place of ideas – that interact with each other. The economic dimension is only one sphere that enables the demonstration of the power of competition as a building mechanism.[6]

The vision of the ideal structure of society as a multi-dimensional competitive market is based upon the perception that in an ideal competitive market the self-interests of individuals are channeled spontaneously, and without their intentions, for the benefit of society. To put it differently, one of the building blocks of the whole configuration are positive unintended consequences. For example, the producer who wishes to maximize profits becomes obligated to take into account the market requirements and therefore must produce quality goods that are in demand.[7] However, this simple insight is only the beginning of a long chain reaction. One of the reasons is that producing quality goods in a competitive environment requires constant development and elaboration. The practical meaning is that even the simplest producer finds himself seeking new knowledge and new knowledge is likely to yield discoveries and innovations that create opportunities in different dimensions of our social and personal life. For example, many innovations that were initially developed for military purposes, such as satellite technology (for example Global Positioning System), are now in use by the general public for civil causes.

The knowledge dimension enables us to go beyond the simple classical economic model of producer and consumer and to view an ideal structure of society as a multidimensional free market that operates as a constructive evolutionary mechanism. The individual's self interest is the dynamo that propels society forward (new knowledge, discoveries, and innovations), and the competition is the regulators – mostly elements that are beneficial for the members of society to survive in the crucible of competition.[8] The question is: Is this vision of competition as a building mechanism realistic or an imaginary fantasy of great naïve thinkers, such as Adam Smith, Friedrich Hayek, and many other protagonists of the free market system?

This book focuses upon an entirely different kind of social competition – intractable conflict. This kind of competition operates differently than the ideal free market system. The general rule that characterizes the evolutionary progression of intractable conflict is – almost any societal element that benefits the conflict survives and whatever operates against it becomes extinct.

The ideal free market system and intractable conflict demonstrate that competition is a powerful force that can operate in opposite directions. It can be manifested as a building mechanism that pushes society forward (the ideal free market system) and it can operate as a destructive instrument that brings misery and despair (intractable conflict): Is it possible to control and maneuver the direction in which social competition pushes society? Is there a way to transform a destructive competition (violent struggle) to a constructive contest (political dispute that leads to agreements and litigation)? How can we ensure that any competitive mechanism leads the evolution of society in the desirable direction?

Constitutional economists, like James Buchanan, are fully aware of the existence of various forms of destructive competition. They emphasize that competition per se tends to create social failures, such as monopolies, and can be the motivating vehicle behind other social disasters, such as civil wars and intractable conflicts. They emphasize that constructive competition, competition that can benefit the members of society, can emerge only in an adequate framework of rules and institutions.[9] To put it differently, the project of constitutional economists is to search for the appropriate rules of the social game that will navigate the competitive social interactions for the benefit of the participants.

In a sports contest, the rules of the game are designed to ensure that the best team will win. In a free society, the rules of the social game and political and social institutions intend to guarantee that the members of society will benefit from the constructive powers of multidimensional competition. To put it differently, an adequate framework of rules and institutions are necessary conditions for creating a peaceful, prosperous, and decent social order.[10]

Rules and institutions are social tools that maneuver, guide and control the social interactions. The rules of the social game are designed to determine what is allowed and what is forbidden in a free society, while social institutions enable the society to function, prosper, and cope with crises. In a free society, social and political institutions maintain and promote the culture of freedom and independence by providing basic mechanisms and services, particularly: instruments to solve disputes by peaceful means (a judiciary system), means to maintain law and order (policing services), resources to educate the people (schools and universities), and tools to operate the economy (such as the banking system).

The social reformer points out that building the foundations of a good society in Israel and the Palestinian territories is necessary to create the conditions for an effective peace process. It can help people to discover the benefit of a peaceful social order, educate them to solve disputes by peaceful means, and strengthen the pro-negotiating elements in the opposing societies. These effects can bring to the stage of politics a new peacemaking social force that is necessary in this situation.[11]

Domestic reforms in Israel and the Palestinian territories are necessary for building an adequate framework that could push the opposing societies to engage again in constructive competition (negotiation by peaceful means). A peace process that does not include domestic reforms within each of the opposing societies is, probably, not going to succeed. The reason is that each one of them will not be prepared to carry the harmful unintended consequences of any peace process.

The tragic history of protracted social conflicts shows that almost any progression toward resolution of the struggle tends to increase violence. Without the social structure that can help the people to cope with this side effect any constructive competition, negotiation by peaceful means, is probably going to collapse again and again into a destructive contest, which leads to unproductive dialogue by violent means.

Promoting peace increases violence

The history of the Palestinian-Israeli struggle shows clearly that almost any substantial progression towards peace is likely to increase the level of violence. We identify two major reasons to this somewhat strange phenomenon. The first is that spoilers increase efforts to sabotage any progress toward a peaceful resolution of the conflict through violence. The second is that any progress towards peace between the two opposing societies tends to create, expose, and increase tensions within each one of them. This is a critical element in a fragile social order – like the one in the Palestinian society – that lacks effective mechanisms to peacefully resolve internal tensions and disputes. Let me elaborate on these two issues.

a. *Professional spoilers, radicals, and extremists*

"Professional" spoilers are societal elements that work in opposition to almost any peaceful negotiations between representatives of the opposing societies and make all efforts to stop them. They could be religious extremists, individuals who see any peace process as a national suicide, and political groups for whom the conflict is a central motif in their identity. The hard core of the spoilers cannot, or are not willing to, make any transition and transformation in their perception.

The phenomenon of spoilers, who are motivated to increase violence in order to wreck the peace process, appears in almost any intractable conflict like the Palestinian-Israeli struggle. For example, violence, in almost any shape, form and version, carried by the enemies of the peace process, appeared during the all-party negotiations in Northern Ireland and the multi-party talks in South Africa. Senator Mitchell, the independent chairman of the peace process in Northern Ireland, described his frustration again and again. For example, when "the all-party talks on the Northern Ireland's future were thrown into disarray . . . after a bomb ripped through a Protestant village minute before the Ulster Unionists were preparing finally to join negotiations," the Senator complained "when I heard the news my heart sank and I thought, Oh God, this is so difficult! Every time we're on the verge of progress, a bomb goes off or someone is shot. Will we ever be able to work it out?"[12]

The violent episodes during the Oslo Accord of the 1990s demonstrate the ability of spoilers to seriously damage almost any Palestinian-Israeli peace process. During the implementation of the initiative and towards negotiations on a final settlement that will put an end to the conflict: suicide bombers frequently blew themselves up inside Israel; the Israeli right-wing opposition to the accord launched a harsh public opinion campaign against the government of Israel; and Yitzhak Rabin, the Israeli Prime Minister, was assassinated by an extremist Jew in 1995.[13]

The continuing of the settlement project (which is considered as Israeli violence by the Palestinians) and Palestinians' ongoing violent attacks against Israeli civilians, only exacerbated the mutual suspicion of the two communities. These episodes, carried out by extremists, demonstrated to each side that the beginning of a new peacemaking chapter in the bloody history of the Palestinian-Israeli conflict is no more than an imaginary fantasy of hallucinating leaders. This effect strengthens the popularity of the hardliners in both societies. Benjamin Netanyahu, a right-wing leader, who opposed the Oslo peace process, won the Israeli general elections and became the Prime Minister of Israel in 1996.[14] The militant Islamist movement Hamas gained more and more popularity in the Palestinian streets.

b. Promoting peace increases tensions within each of the opposing societies

Each society is a composite of different societal elements: individuals, political parties, religious factions, ethnic groups, and so on. These various social entities do not necessarily share the same viewpoints, priorities, preferences, and political agenda. Intractable conflict, which is central to the experience of almost anyone in the opposing societies, is a unified force. Adversaries may join forces to fight a joint enemy and collaborate in order to change a miserable situation that is considered to be a threat for their existence, identity, and dignity. However, as soon as there is substantial progress towards a resolution of the struggle, tensions within each society appears and starts playing a dominant role: Is the peace process a positive change or an existential threat? What are the features, shape, and structure of our future political and social system going to be: democracy, religious autocracy, power sharing, or any other option? Who are going to be our allies: the Arab countries, the US, the European Union, or maybe China?

Any progression toward a beneficial change in the political order has side effects that can damage the whole process. For example, the Apartheid in South Africa had united the non-white populations and made the struggle look like "a black-versus-white one." However, the progression toward a new social order exposed the diversity within the non-white population and led to violent clashes between different factions in the "black" camp.[15]

Transition and transformation from one structure to another require adequate political mechanisms that can help society to survive the shock. The unilateral withdrawal of the Israeli forces from Gaza, which was led by the Israeli Prime Minister Ariel Sharon in 2005, demonstrates the difficulties and the obstacles. Ironically, the developments were quite different than one might expect.

Sharon's plan to withdraw all Israeli troops and about 8,000 Jewish settlers from Gaza and four small areas in the West Bank did not accrue in a vacuum. For a long time, there was a growing consensus among the Israelis that occupation of Gaza is hopeless, useless, and too expensive. However, on the other hand, the massive and uncompromising campaign that the settlers and their supporters led against Sharon's plan gave the impression that it is not going to be easy to pull back from Gaza. The people in Israel were afraid that any evacuation of Jewish settlements from Gaza had the potential to start a civil war within Israel.

There is no doubt that the unilateral withdrawal left an open wound in Israeli society. However, Israel continued to exist as a unified country but the Palestinian authority was the one that collapsed. The events that followed were a bloody civil war within Palestinian society and a coup d'état by Hamas in Gaza.

The different effects of the unilateral withdrawal on the two societies are not surprising for students of social affairs. There is a big difference between Israel and the Palestinian authority. Israel is an established state with effective mechanisms that can maintain law and order and solve internal tensions, disputes, and controversies by democratic means. The Palestinian authority is a developing entity that lacks the instruments to cope with the social crises that can follow a dramatic transition from one political order to another.

The transitional period in developing countries that lack effective mechanisms to maintain law and order, is a trigger that can lead to social crises, catastrophes, and collapse. The short history of the Palestinian authority resembles the political evolution of the modernizing countries of Asia, Africa, and Latin America after World War II, as described by Samuel Huntington:

> increasing ethnic and class conflict, recurring rioting and mob violence, frequent military coups d'état, the dominance of unstable personalistic leaders who often pursued disastrous economic and social policies, widespread and blatant corruption among cabinet ministers and civil servants, arbitrary infringement of the rights and liberties of citizens, declining standards of bureaucratic efficiency and performance, the pervasive alienation of urban political groups, the loss of authority by legislatures and courts, and the fragmentation and at times complete disintegration of broadly based political parties."[16]

The transformation period is very fragile, sensitive, and a dangerous situation for modernizing societies. Transforming from occupation to independence, or more precisely semi-independence (Gaza is under seize by Israel and Egypt), can quite easily deteriorate into chaos (a failed social order that cannot provide basic needs to the people). The lack of constructive means to stabilize the new situation tends to strengthen the dark forces in society that unite the suffering people by the usual means of hate and incitement. This internal collapse can lead to escalation in external conflict, such as the crisis between Hamas in Gaza and Israel toward the end of 2008.

The social reformer argues that the success of peacemaking policy that intends to resolve conflict between opposing societies, depends on the political structure within each one of them. The effectiveness of political institutions is necessary to implement agreements and make the transition from a conflict situation to a peaceful social order possible. Each of the opposing societies needs a clear strategy for domestic reforms.

A domestic strategy that can give a melodic line to the decisions of policy makers is necessary to start improving the social and political conditions in the opposing societies. Unfortunately, both Israel and Palestinian society have suffered from chronic ambivalence in their political system which was discovered as a major obstacle for peace.

Political ambivalence versus political strategy

Society, especially in times of crisis and transition, needs political strategy to cope with the challenges. An ideal political strategy gives direction and melodic line to political moves but, at the same time, is flexible enough to be changed according to the ongoing unexpected developments.[17] Unfortunately, the political system of Israel and the Palestinian authority have been far from reaching this ideal.

A chronic ambivalence has characterized the function of the Israeli political system following the 1967 war and the new emerging Palestinian authority. Israel did not have a clear strategy to cope with the future of the territories captured in the 1967 war[18] and Palestinian politics have been marred by ambivalence between democratic aspirations and Islamist autocracy.[19]

A chronic ambivalence in politics, especially in a pressing situation that demands a clear political strategy, can be very dangerous and costly. It gives a precious opportunity to radicals, who have a clear political agenda, to dictate conditions to the rest of the people. Thus, the settlement project was born in a political vacuum after the 1967 war and the radical Islamist movement Hamas accumulated political and militaristic power since its establishment at the beginning of the first Palestinian *Intifada* in 1987. These two political trends, among the many other complicated problems, made sure that an effective peace process would look like an impossible mission. Following the Oslo Accord of the 1990s, the settlement project did not stop growing and expanding in the disputed territories, while the Palestinian leaders found major difficulties in fulfilling their commitment to stop violent attacks inside Israel and end incitement. These critical elements contradicted the logic, spirit, and understanding of the historical accord.

Creating facts – the settlement project

The occupation of the West Bank and the Gaza strip made the "Palestinian problem" an internal problem of Israel. Israel, on the one hand, had more defensible borders and maybe better opportunities to try and stop Palestinian insurgencies. However, on the other hand, 1.3 million Palestinians were living under a militaristic occupation by a state that is considered to be almost the only democracy in the region.

The government of Israel did not have a clear program for dealing with the occupied territories. There were many suggestions on how to cope with the new situation but not a clear decision, strategy, and political program.[20] The settlements were born in this political vacuum. The beginning of the settlement project in the disputed territories was a few Jewish outposts mostly in strategic places for strategic and militaristic considerations.[21] However, very soon ideology started to play a major role and few strategic outposts turned into a whole project. The motivation was to fulfill the old messianic dream of greater Israel – the Biblical Promised Land.

The settlers had a clear strategy – settling in the occupied territories and creating facts on the ground. The idea that controlling the land means political power was not invented by the settlers. The political program of the first Zionist Congress, at the beginning of the twentieth century, was based on the same logic. The strategy was purchasing land in swampy Palestine and building a home for the Jewish people.[22] There can be no doubt that the Zionist political program helped to establish the state of Israel. However, the question is: Is the strategy of "settling and creating facts," which helped in the creation of the new Jewish state before 1948, suitable for the occupied territories after 1967?

One does not need to be a professional political scientist to see that building settlements in the disputed territories is extremely problematic, especially from a Jewish-Israeli perspective. For example, it seems to be impossible to create a Jewish majority in the territories, at least by peaceful means (the demographic argument). Ariel Sharon, when he became the Prime Minister of Israel in 2001, understood it very well, at least in regard to Gaza. The architect of the settlement project understood that his original strategy of trying to swamp the land with Jewish settlers failed (ironically, the Palestinians had more children). At the end of the day, maintaining the settlement project in Gaza is too costly in all aspects and it is not going to bring much benefit. The Prime Minister dramatically changed his strategy and decided to dismantle the settlements and to pull back from the Gaza strip.

In general, it is easier to replace one strategy with another rather than to come up with a clear political program out of a steady situation of chronic political ambiguity.[23] Indeed, Sharon changed his strategy by putting an end to the endless discussion upon the burden of maintaining a hopeless occupation in the Gaza strip and evacuated the area; Menachem Begin, following Sadat's dramatic initiative, changed his uncompromising strategy by giving back Egyptian territories captured in the Six-Day War in return for a peace treaty. Unfortunately, Israeli politics has suffered from chronic ambiguity in regard to the future of the West Bank. The lack of a clear strategy on how to cope with a situation of endless occupation, has enabled the radicals, who have a clear political program, to create facts that can bring disaster to their society.

The growing and expansion of the Jewish settlements in the West Bank has imposed constraints and limitations upon any future negotiation. There are major settlement blocks, such as Ariel, Ma'ale Adumim, and Gush Etzion, which are almost impossible to evacuate and dismantle. The practical meaning is that land swap will have to be seriously considered in any serious negotiation that is based on the two state solution and the 1967 cease-fire line. For example, some of the settlement blocks will remain under Israeli sovereignty and in return, Israel will give the Palestinians the same amount of land in quantity and quality.[24]

However, the situation is not static. More and more settlements are built and settlers try to create a situation where it will be impossible to dismantle them. A rapid growing and expansion of the settlement project leads to a point where the "two state solution" is not going to be a viable option any more. Our social-reformer does not hesitate in insisting and asking: Which direction is Israel is going to take? How to cope with a situation of an ongoing occupation that leads to an unending struggle? Is there any peacemaking strategy behind the settlement project?

The ongoing continuation of the settlement project, eventually, can lead to the point where the "two state solution" is not going to be a feasible option anymore. "One state solution" is the nightmare of the majority of Jewish Israelis. Jewish Israelis are convinced that one state for the two people means the loss of Jewish majority in Israel and the destruction of the only Jewish state in the world. Again, what are the options?

The "one state solution" is not an option (the majority of Jewish Israelis object). The "two state solution" is not going to be an option (if the settlement project will continue to grow). To "peacefully" continue the occupation until the end of history is probably not going to work either. So, where Israel is going to? What is the future of the Jewish state? How to cope with the growing Palestinian problem?

Many settlers are strong believers in God. They probably expect that a "reasonable" solution will occur from heaven or, at least, they believe that settling in the Biblical Israel is a divine obligation that every Jew has to follow without raising any doubts. However, most of the people in Israel are secular and do not believe in miracles. But still it looks like Israel does not have a clear strategy on how to cope with this complicated issue. The result can be disaster.

The ongoing occupation, with all its implications, affects almost all aspects of social life in Israel. An effective domestic strategy will have to cope with the question of how to build the foundations of a peaceful social order. It has to put on the Israeli public agenda possibilities for resolving the struggle: one state, two states, three states, federation, confederation, or any other possibility. However, the next question is: Is the Israeli political system built to carry a change in the political attitude toward such an existential problem?[25]

The problem of adaptability

The survival of social organization is dependent upon its ability to cope with challenges, changes, and crises. Political institutions (that operate the organization) and the rules of the game (which determine what is allowed and what is forbidden) are political tools that enable the organization to function. The lack of efficient tools, rules, and institutions, damages the ability of the organization to function properly and to respond to new challenges. The political systems of Israel and the Palestinian authorities have suffered from chronic maladies that were discovered as major obstacles for peace.

The parliamentary structure of Israel is based on a multi-party system. No political party has ever succeeded in gaining the necessary majority of votes to establish a government by itself alone. Most Israeli governments were dependent on partnerships and coalitions with minor religious parties. To put it differently, the fate of almost every Israeli government has been determined by the rise and fall in the votes of these parties.

One manifestation of this distortion (the major role that minor religious parties played in Israeli politics) is the expansion of the settlement project. For example, personal political ambitions motivated the former Minister of Defense Shimon Peres, who is considered to be a visionary peacemaker, to support the establishment of approximately 85 new settlements in the occupied territories, between 1975 and 1977.[26]

It took many years for Ariel Sharon – a strong, skillful and tactician politician – to become the Prime Minister of Israel. Sharon, who knew very well how to play and manipulate the system, established a broad coalition and led a unilateral historic Israeli withdrawal from Gaza.[27] Sharon led this dramatic move, which reflected the preferences of most Israeli voters, in spite of the resistance of the majority of his traditional right-wing supporters.[28]

The problematic parliamentary system of Israel demonstrates that decent democracy requires constant development and elaboration of democratic procedures. Palestinian politics reminds us once again that democracy is not necessarily equivalent to democratic elections.[29] In 2006 the Palestinians conducted an impressive legislative election. However, the results contradicted the spirit of almost any decent democracy. The radical Islamist party, Hamas, won the majority of seats and their leader, Ismail Haniya, was called to form a government.

The Palestinian people forgot, or maybe did not take intoaccount, that giving the majority of seats to an anti-democratic party is, usually, an irreversible choice. It is almost impossible to replace an autocratic regime, which used and abused democratic procedures to get elected, by another democratic election. The question is: What was the alternative?

The Palestinian authority suffered from major problems and failures that characterized many other developing countries. Among the "classical" symptoms, we can clearly identify dysfunctioning of the governing system and widespread and blatant corruption among the representatives of the ruling secular party, Fatah. The ongoing occupation and the expansion of the settlement project did not give much comfort to the Palestinian people either. The result was escapism into the illusionary relaxation that religion has to offer.

As Freud, Marx, and many other scholars have pointed out, misery and despair are fertile ground to capture the hearts and minds of distressed people by offering them divine salvation. In this case, it was not only imagination but a pure reality. The Islamic socio-political organization Hamas built an impressive network for delivering charity and education that alleviated the misery of the Palestinian people.

The 2006 election for the Palestinian Legislative Council was an opportunity for the Palestinian people to punish the corrupted regime of the secular Fatah and to reword the religious party Hamas that offered them social services. However, the Palestinian people seem to ignore the fact that the Hamas regime is a whole package deal that does not include only charity and social services. Hamas, the Palestinian branch of the Muslim Brotherhood, has a clear political agenda that is based on radical elements such as: creating Islamic autocracy, launching a holy war against Israel and establishing a global pan Islamic state.[30] Public surveys show that most of the Palestinian people, religious and secular, do not share this kind of political aspiration. The Palestinians' strong desire for a positive change in their political system trapped them in a situation that seems to worsen their position.

Two political forces in Palestinian society

Palestinian society has been teetering between two major forces – the secular movement PLO and the radical Islamist party Hamas. The leadership of each one of them is committed to a different ideology and political agenda. The PLO is a secular nationalist movement that is striving to develop the foundations of a civil society in the Palestinian territories. The agenda of Hamas, the militant outgrowth of the Muslim Brotherhood, is to establish an Islamic autocracy on the whole territory of the holy land.

The tension between secularism and religious fanaticism in the Arab world was not invented in the Palestinian territories. The split in the Palestinian society can be viewed as an offspring of the tension between major trends in the Arab world: Pan-Arabism and Islamism. This tension reached its peak after the age of colonialism when the Arab world had to struggle with the burden of freedom, independence and responsibility.

The pan-Arabism movement – with its champion Gamal Abdul Nasser, the former President of Egypt, who assumed power in 1955 – emphasizes the importance of the ethnic dimension (Arab), while the Islamist movement indentified the term "national identity" with the religious dimension (Islam). The meaning of pan-Arabism is that the Arab people, who are residents in different countries, belong to one nation – the Arab nation (Arab nationalism), while the Islamists support the unity of Muslims under one Islamic state (religious nationalism).[31]

Nasser's main political goals were to remove Western influence from the Middle East and create an Arab bloc that could compete with western capitalism and soviet socialism.[32] The existence of a western Jewish state in the Middle East symbolized for him the extension of western colonialism on Arab soil. Nasser became the symbol of the dream to create a single Arab state, stretching from the Atlantic Ocean to the Persian Gulf, and the struggle against all forms of "Colonialism, Imperialism and Zionism."[33]

The Six-Day War in 1967 and the peace treaty between Israel and Egypt in 1979 are considered as benchmarks in the collapse of the pan-Arabism dream. Two significant results were the Palestinization of the Arab-Israeli conflict and the rise of radical Islam.[34] These two political trends influenced the internal politics of Palestinian society.

The Palestinization of the Arab-Israeli conflict means that the Palestinians became the significant actor in the confrontation. Major trends in the region – such as the inability of the Arab states to defeat Israel, the lack of Arab commitment to the Palestinians' causes, and the "new" Israeli occupation – taught the Palestinians that they need to take their faith in their own hands. The Palestinians became the major force responsible to fight for their own objectives.[35]

The search of the Palestinians for pragmatic tools (militaristic and diplomatic) to cope with their problems and suffering contributed to the consolidation of a Palestinian national-secular identity. From pragmatic consideration, the goal slowly became to establish an independent Palestinian state in Gaza and the West Bank (the territories which were captured by Israel in the 1967 war). In contrast, the ideologists of Hamas, the militant outgrowth of the Muslim Brotherhood, have seen in the liberation of all mandatory Palestine an important milestone in the road to establish a pan-Islamic state. Holy war and the establishment of an Islamic autocracy in Palestine is only one step in the struggle to achieve the final goal.

The operation of the Muslim Brotherhood, the Islamic movement that created Hamas, in the holy land started in 1947, when the Brotherhood founded its first branch in Jerusalem. Their main activity focused upon building the foundations of an Islamic state through charity organizations, religious institutions, and Islamic education. After the 1967 war, the Brotherhood refrained from active resistance to the Israeli occupation in the West Bank and Gaza and continued to prepare the Islamic revolution. Their grassroots activities enabled them to gain popularity in the Palestinian streets and build a power base in Palestinian society. However, their refusal to take part in resisting the occupation caused them to lose supporters to the competitive PLO, the Palestinian secular national movement, and later to the Islamic Jihad, another offshoot of the Muslim Brotherhood.[36]

The turning point in the struggle upon the identity, image and structure of the Palestinian society was the first *Intifada* in 1987. The growing nationalist sentiments of the Palestinians made the leadership of the Brotherhood understand that they need to change their policy. The result was the establishment of Hamas, the militant outgrowth of the Muslim Brotherhood.[37]

The agenda of Hamas is holy war against the Jewish state, establishing an Islamic autocracy in the holy land and participating in a global effort to create a pan-Islamic state. The "new" ideology has enabled Hamas to become a major political and militaristic power in the Palestinian society.

The Oslo Accord of the 1990s was a precious opportunity for Yasser Arafat, the leader of the secular PLO, who was in the exile, to go back to the Palestinian territories and start to implement the secular agenda of his organization. Arafat and his associates received financial and militaristic support to start building the foundations of a good society. However, Arafat the revolutionary was discovered to be a failure as a state builder.[38] In contrast to the Machiavellian prince, the founder of a new social order, Arafat's style of leadership contributed to the split inPalestinian society that reached its peak in the brutal coup d'état of Hamas in Gaza after Arafat's death in 2007.

The social reformer emphasizes that the split in Palestinian society – Gaza and the West Bank – is not only territorial, but also ideological and political. The secular regime in the West Bank is committed to build an independent Palestinian civil society based on the 1967 cease-fire line ("two state solution"). Hamas in Gaza is committed to build an Islamic autocracy in all of Mandatory Palestine, which is considered to be an Islamic *waqf* (property).

The ideologists of Hamas see in any territorial compromise with Israel a religious sin.[39]

The social reformer searches for opportunities for domestic reforms to improve the situation of the Palestinians. However, there is a big difference between Gaza and the West Bank. Conducting domestic reforms in Gaza, at this stage, is extremely difficult, but implementing domestic reforms in the West Bank is possible and an urgent necessity at this stage. Helping the Palestinians to build the foundations of a good society in the West Bank should take first priority. Domestic reforms in the West Bank can have direct and indirect influence upon the social-political situation: weakening the radical elements in the West Bank; encouraging and strengthening the moderate elements in Gaza (Hamas is not one voice); giving hope to the Palestinian people (most of them, according to public surveys, do not share the aspirations of Hamas) and building the foundations for a peace process with Israel.

Religion, identity, and decent Israel

The difficult task of creating opportunities for peacemaking requires preparing the opposing societies, Palestinians and Israelis, for coexistence. This means that domestic reforms in Palestinian society are not enough to build the foundations for an effective peace process. There is a need for domestic reforms within the state of Israel, especially, in regard to the sensitive issue of "national identity" and its practical implications.

Israel is a multicultural society. The Israeli population includes a majority of Jewish citizens who came from different parts of the world and a large minority of non-Jewish citizens (about 25 percent Arabs). Nevertheless, Israel is considered to be a Jewish state. One of the manifestations of "Jewish state" is the lack of clear separation between state and rabbinic institutions. A good example is the "Law of Return" which gives Jews and their families the right to immigrate, settle in Israel, and get Israeli citizenship with full rights and obligations. The label "Jewish state" and its practical implications put the non-Jewish Israeli population in a difficult position.

True, a major part of the Arab-Israelis' integration in the Israeli society is expressed through participation of the Arab population in the democratic processes of Israel.[40] Nevertheless, the fact that a non-Jewish population belongs to a Jewish state enfolds many elements of exclusion. The politics of exclusion is expressed in many dimensions of the Israeli social life, for example the psychological dimension (many Arab-Israelis see themselves as second-class citizens) and the symbolic sphere (the national symbols of the country are taken from Jewish tradition).

A good society requires constant development, improvement, and elaboration of effective procedures and mechanisms that are designed to address the need of the people. A modern Israel needs solutions to reduce tensions between "Israel as a democratic state" and "Israel as a Jewish state." To put it differently, there is a need to diminish tensions between democratic values (such as equality) and the need of Jewish people to own a small piece of land. A realistic vision of a modern and decent Israel would require Israelis, Jews and non Jews, to think practically, and not only theoretically, about better accommodation of ethnic minorities in the state of Israel and in Israeli society.[41]

The existence of Arab citizens in Israel has many important effects upon the conduct of the country in general and its relation with the Palestinians in the territories in particular.[42] Improved relations between the Jewish majority and the Arab minority in Israel might pave the way for better relations with a future Palestinian polity and create opportunities for conflict resolution. It can help the Jewish population in Israel to overcome the obsessive fear of losing the Jewish character of the country. The implications can be substantial and dramatic. For example, the people in Israel might be more receptive to seriously examine creative solutions to the conflict and, even, consider including Arab representatives in Israeli delegations for future negotiations. A trust building domestic policy can create precious opportunities for peacemaking, peace building, and peacekeeping.

Summary

Transition from one state to another is difficult for almost any society. A transitional period for developing entities, which have hardly developed political and social mechanisms to cope with new challenges, can end in disaster. Huntington pointed out that the lack of an effective framework of rules and institutions in changing societies can be used and abused by a new social force to take control. The new political player who comes to power is not necessarily able, interested, or knows how to establish the foundations of a new social order that can benefit the members of society.

The logic of the Oslo peace process of the 1990s was to gradually implement the idea of a "two state solution". The reality was that the Palestinian authority teetered between one crisis and another. Unfortunately, the victory of Hamas in the election for the Palestinian Legislative Council was only one element in a long chain of disasters.

The social-reformer model is a conflict-management strategy that intends to put boundaries and limitations to the conflict. The idea is to manage the conflict by offering domestic reforms to each of the opposing societies. Building the foundations of a good society in Israel and the Palestinian disputed territories can diminish the impact of intensified conflict by reducing the influence of extremists, helping the people to discover the value of peace, and inviting a substantial peacemaking force to appear on the stage of Middle East politics.

The assumption of the social reformer is that it should be in the best interests of the majority of the people on both sides to end the conflict by peaceful means. However, the Palestinian-Israeli conflict clearly demonstrates that promoting the self-interest of human beings can be a very difficult mission.[43] Indeed, the Palestinians and the Israelis are engaged in a frustrating intractable conflict that neither can win. The Palestinians will probably not be able to dismantle the state of Israel and the Israelis cannot maintain the occupation forever and stop Palestinian insurgencies by militaristic moves. This trivial observation, which is probably well known to most of the people, did not help, so far, to promote the culture of peace.

From every reasonable perspective, it should be the self-interest of the two communities to transform the destructive competition, the endless violent dialogue, to a constructive contest, which means negotiation by peaceful means.[44] However, constructive and effective competition that brings out the best in self-interested human beings can emerge only in a stable framework of rules and institutions. Without the social foundations for a new social order the two societies will not be able to cope with difficulties, crises, and problems that almost any effective peace process tends to invite (such as increasing violence).

The social reformer points out that domestic reforms in each of the opposing societies is a precondition to a successful peace process. The two societies need a clear domestic agenda sufficiently coherent and flexible for inevitable and ad hoc revisions and corrections.[45] It is recommended that domestic strategies for the two societies, Israeli and Palestinian, will address the following issues:

- *State building* – establishing the foundations of a modern free independent state in the Palestinian territories: building public institutions, creating a stable and transparent administration, disarming violent groups, and developing civil society.
- *Democracy* – improving the democratic features of Israel: reforming the parliamentary system which enables minorities to dictate conditions to the rest of the people, reducing the tensions between state and religious institutions, better accommodating the non-Jewish minorities.
- *Economy* – building a viable Palestinian economy that provides employment to the people and is less dependent on foreign aid.
- *Education* – stopping incitement, educating for peace, and learning the tradition, culture, and history of the other.
- *Media* – putting the emphasis on state building and peacemaking efforts and marginalizing the focus on violent episodes of extremists.

Ironically, the focus upon domestic reforms within each society helps to better understand the impact and influence of the conflict upon all walks of life. To put it differently, it is impossible to build the foundations of a decent Israeli society and a decent Palestinian one without resolving the conflict between them. Domestic strategies that intend to improve the position of each society need to offer practical moves to progress the culture of peace.

This way of thinking demonstrates that the Palestinian domestic difficulties are not only an internal Palestinian problem. It is also an Israeli problem and a regional problem. It is in the best interests of Israelis and major Arab countries, such as Egypt and Jordan, to help the Palestinians establish a viable stable polity that could stop the expansion and flourishing of religious fanaticism.

Realizing the regional interest to stabilize the social situation in Palestinian society brings into consideration different types of regional arrangements that include multiple players, such as federation and confederation. However, big dreams require small practical steps. The social-reformer's point of departure is to offer domestic reforms in the most urgent places where the circumstances permit – the state of Israel and the Palestinian administration in the West Bank. The intention is to create peacemaking hope in the West Bank that could be transmitted to the people in Gaza and to block the desperation in Gaza from expanding into the West Bank.[46]

To conclude, the social reformer model encourages domestic reforms within each of the opposing societies in order to create the foundations for a peaceful social order. Like the strong-leader model, the social-reformer model offers a strategy to change the political structure of the conflict. Its main weakness is that it does not address the conflict directly and cannot sustain a peace process by itself. It is an unrealistic utopia to believe that an effective resolution to the conflict will emerge, spontaneously, out of domestic reforms within Israel and the Palestinian society. However, the social-reformer model introduces necessary domestic moves that should accompany any peace process. In the worst-case scenario, the social-reformer model will help to ensure that if the peace process fails, the results will not be as catastrophic for either side as they have been in the recent past.

6 The political-elite model

Introduction

Two critical elements are necessary to build the foundations for an effective peace process in a complicated situation like the Palestinian-Israeli struggle: peacemaking leaders and the preparation of the opposing societies for an effective peace process. These two elements are intertwined. Peacemaking leaders need the peoples' support to deliver their agenda. People that are eager for a reasonable peace process are likely to invite peacemaking leaders to the stage of politics and demand substantial progression in the direction of peace. The question is: How to create this circulating structure?

Two competitive models can be useful in building the foundations for revolutionary relationships between the opposing societies: the political-elite and the public-assembly. The political-elite model offers various forms of interactions between political elites from both sides as the dominant method in the Palestinian-Israeli struggle. The public-assembly model, which is new in the region, proposes to establish a major Palestinian-Israeli public-assembly – a public negotiating congress. The vision of this peace-building institution is loosely based upon the multi-party talks that helped to create dramatic change in two other desperate situations of intractable conflict: Apartheid South-Africa and Northern-Ireland during the "troubles."

I suggest regarding these two competitive models as complementary. The political-elite model is mainly designed to begin a peace process, support it, and finalize a peace agreement. The public-assembly model intends to involve the people in the peacemaking process and to help them discover the road to replace violent sentiments with peaceful bargaining, debate, and critical discussion.

The political-elite and the public-assembly are conflict-resolution models. Negotiation in different versions, forms, and dimensions plays a key role in each one of them. They are designed to cope with the core issues of the conflict head-on and to build relationships between the two sides.

The political-elite model

The political-elite model offers various forms of interaction between political-elites from both sides and it is the dominant peacemaking experience in the Middle East. This model has been tried and implemented in almost infinite shapes, forms, and variations in Middle East politics in general and the Palestinian-Israeli struggle in particular. In its classical forms the political-elite model includes three major modes of interactions: track II diplomacy, secret diplomacy, and track I diplomacy.[1]

Track II diplomacy involves informal study, exploration and bargaining between wide circles of unofficial political-elites, such as: businessmen, academic scholars, journalists, and retired politicians. The main purpose is to explore opportunities for peacefully resolving the conflict and prepare the actual negotiation. Secret diplomacy mainly involves secret negotiations between official representatives of opposing leaderships aimed at sketching principles and general guidelines for the official negotiation and the final peace pact. Track I diplomacy is the formal negotiation between official representatives of both sides where, generally, agreements are worked out.

The political-elite model is a broad concept made up of various combinations of these interactions. It intends to provide optimal conditions to reach a peace pact.

Three diplomatic channels of peacemaking

Track II diplomacy is the most interesting and delicate channel of communication in the classic form of the political-elite model. It involves informal discussion, research, and exploration between unofficial elites from both sides. Its aims are to understand the difficulties of the other side, to discuss unpopular and creative ideas, and to prepare the actual negotiation.[2]

To achieve the maximum benefit from the interaction, the participants in track II diplomacy are usually "mid-level" elites. This means that they have to obtain a social status of political–elites but they cannot have an official position in the government. Examples of "mid-level" political-elites can be: retired politicians, senior journalists, scholars, businessmen, and former military generals.

The mid-level status of the participants in track II diplomacy (unofficial political-elites) has advantages on two levels. On the one hand, their unofficial status gives them more space to maneuver and a great degree of freedom to explore creative and sometimes unpopular ideas. On the other hand, their elite status and connections are supposed to help them in transferring knowledge gained from the interaction to current leaders and policy makers. In an ideal track II interaction, the participants are able to: think "outside of the box" and come up with innovative insights for making changes in a desperate situation of intractable conflict; to share the new ideas with influential policy makers; and to shape the public opinion by civil activities, such as: giving lectures, writing newspaper articles, and publishing books.

To achieve maximum results from track II diplomacy and to approach the ideal, the participants have to be chosen carefully. Past experience shows that in almost any track II interaction there are tensions and substantial gaps between the ability to conduct a fruitful, beneficial, and productive interaction and the possibilities of transferring the results to the leadership and, especially, to the general public.[3] The failure of "Project Charlie," which was born as result of the Oslo peace process of the 1990s, demonstrates this tension.

The Oslo Accord of 1993 gave the impression that the Israeli government and the PLO leadership were marching hand in hand toward the implementation of a two-state solution. The settlers who lived in the disputed territories felt a major concern for their future. On the one hand, they advocated an uncompromising position against the accord and led a massive campaign against the Israeli government. However, on the other hand, there was an urgent need to make some preparations for the worst-case scenario – the establishment of an independent Palestinian state. Among the important questions that needed clarification were: How did the Palestinian leadership envision a situation where Jewish settlers were living under their control? Who is going to take responsibility in a case of emergency, Israel or the Palestinians? How to oppose the Oslo Accord without leading to an uncontrolled chain of escalation and violence?

Back channel diplomacy was the perfect track to explore these critical questions without damaging the official settlers' uncompromised objection and rejection of the Oslo Accord. "Project Charlie" is the name code for secret track II meetings between unofficial representatives of the Jewish settlers and the Palestinians that took place mostly in mid-1995.[4]

Newspaper reports that exposed the talks put a lot of pressure on the Israeli participants and the meetings were stopped.[5] Ironically, the project gave the impression, to the Israeli public, that if the train of peace is going to accelerate in the direction of a two state solution, the settlers, who are considered as hardliners and a major obstacle for peace, might join the accord and accept a reasonable compromise. This was one of the unintended consequences of track II talks, which were designed to explore possibilities for a desperate scenario from the settlers' point of view.[6]

Secret diplomacy suggests peacemaking interactions between officials from both sides that is totally excluded from the public and the media. It can be viewed as an intermediate channel of elite's communication between informal settings (track II diplomacy) and the official negotiation (track I

diplomacy). Secret diplomacy is a useful peacemaking tool for the preparation of a dramatic political move when the conditions for involving the local
and international communities are not ready yet.

Usually, drastic political moves that lead to a dramatic shift in the relations between opponents do not occur in a vacuum. They need some kind of
preparation in order to minimize chances of failure. Indeed, prior to Sadat's
diplomatic offensive in 1977, Moshe Dayan, the Israeli Foreign Minister, met
secretly in Morocco with Egyptian Deputy Prime Minister Hassan Tuhamy.[7]
Another example is the secret mission of America's Foreign Minister Henry
Kissinger to Communist China in July 1971, which paved the way for the
historic visit of President Nixon and a dramatic shift in the relationships
between the two countries.[8]

In classical literature of international relations, secret diplomacy is a
broad concept that is not necessarily associated with peacemaking, to say
the very least. It is a diplomatic tool that can be used to advance decent and
indecent political causes.[9] Traditionally, elites always negotiated secretly
and, even, kept their agreements concealed until implementation or viola-
tion was required.[10] Middle East politics is not exceptional.

During the First World War, the British played a double game. They gave
an unofficial commitment, to help in establishing an independent Arab state
after the defeat of the Turks.[11] This political move was intended to guarantee
the Arab revolt against the Ottoman Empire. However, at the same time the
British and the French concluded a secret agreement, known as the Sykes–
Picot Agreement, about the division of control between themselves after the
expected defeat of the Turks.[12]

In retrospect, it is hard to believe that the Sykes–Picot Agreement reflects
the pure peacemaking intentions of the British and the French. To put it
differently, conducting a peaceful social order, which is based on justice
and goodwill, was probably not the main concern of the architects of the
Sykes–Picot Agreement. One of the main lessons is that secret diplomacy is
designed to minimize any objections to promoting a political agenda that is
controversial and might receive substantial resistance.

In the fragile situation of the Middle East, secret diplomacy can be a very
useful peacemaking tool. For example, King Hussein of Jordan had secretly
negotiated with the Israelis long before the official negotiations began and
a peace treaty was signed in 1994. The King, who remembered very well
the assassination of King Abdullah, his moderate grandfather, who stood for
peace with Israel, was very cautious with his political moves. The fact that
Jordan is surrounded by stronger Arab countries hostile to Israel and a major
part of the population is Palestinian were both understood as major obstacles for peace. No doubt the peace agreement between Egypt (the strongest Arab country in the region) and Israel in 1979, and the Oslo Accord

of 1993 (a serious attempt to implement the idea of a two state solution to the Palestinian-Israeli struggle) provided a safety framework for negotiating and concluding a peace agreement between Israel and Jordan.

Track I diplomacy is the official negotiation between representatives of the opposing societies where, generally, agreements are finalized. For example, the Camp David Accord in 1978 where US President Jimmy Carter brokered an agreement between Israeli Prime minister Menachem Begin and Egyptian President Anwar Sadat.

In order to maximize results, the official negotiations (track I diplomacy) have to be carefully prepared. It can be prepared and supported by back channel diplomacy (track II and secret talks). And it could be initiated by a dramatic move of one of the parties that succeeds in creating local and international support. Sadat's offensive diplomacy succeeded in pushing a right-wing Israeli government to the corner. His astonishing arrival in Jerusalem in 1977 succeeded in capturing the hearts of the Israeli public and garnered Western support for an effective accord. However, there is a limit to the influence of one astonishing diplomatic initiative. After Sadat's dramatic move the two sides were still far away from reaching an agreement. It took many efforts and extensive formal negotiations to conclude a peace pact. Carter, as a mediator, played an active role in the negotiating process by putting a lot of pressure on the two sides.

An effective use of the political-elite model is a gradual process that includes the three diplomatic channels. Let me sketch an ideal structure of the model.

From problem-solving to bargaining

Literature on negotiation theory focuses upon two competitive paradigms: bargaining versus problem-solving.[13] The advocates of the bargaining paradigm view negotiation as a competitive interaction where each side makes efforts to advance and defend its own best interests. The supporters of the problem-solving paradigm look at negotiating interaction as a joint effort of conflicting parties to conclude an agreement that could address their fears and needs "on a basis of reciprocity."[14] The questions are: Are those two paradigms necessarily in opposition? Is it possible to create a mechanism that implements insights from the two paradigms in a unitary form? Can we look at these two competitive approaches as complementary?

The various channels of the political-elite model point out that problem-solving and bargaining are more like ideal types that do not really exist in reality. The reason is that almost any peacemaking problem-solving process involves bargaining elements and vice versa. Almost any bargaining procedure involves problem-solving elements. These ideal types, bargaining and problem solving, help us to sketch the spectrum of the peacemaking political-elite's interactions.

Track II diplomacy, unofficial interactions between political-elites, usually, do not have any obligatory status. These interactions are mainly dependent on the good will of the participants who wish to explore opportunities to advance the culture of peace. Therefore, in ideal circumstances, the interaction resembles a problem-solving workshop where the participants join forces and search for solutions to difficult situations of social crisis. The initial stage of the Oslo Accord (track II diplomacy), which is described in the next section, has characteristics of problem-solving engagement: secrecy, unofficial status, and mediation of a third party (Norwegian) which did not have leverage and direct interest in the Middle East.[15]

In contrast, track I diplomacy is the place where agreements are determined and finalized. During the process, policy makers, from both sides, try to improve their position and show that they are doing their best to defend the interests of their people. Accordingly, the interaction looks more like a bargaining process. The Camp David Accord of 1978 had the basic characteristics of a bargaining process: status – the process was official; participants: state leaders (Begin, Sadat, and Carter); mediator: the President of the United States who had leverage and direct interest in the region.[16]

Secret diplomacy is an intermediate stage, in which insights from the unofficial process (track II diplomacy) are transferred to the official negotiations (track I diplomacy). Secret diplomacy interactions have some kind of official status because they involve officials, however, the secrecy gives the participants a greater degree of freedom than the representatives in the actual negotiation (track I diplomacy). The practical meaning is that secret diplomacy is a set of combinations between bargaining and problem-solving.

The Oslo peace process of the 1990s is a unique example that resembles an ideal structure of the political-elite model.

The Oslo Accord – an academic laboratory for peacemaking

The political-elite model is made up of combinations of the three main peacemaking forms of interactions that have been described: track II diplomacy, secret diplomacy, and track I diplomacy. The Oslo Accord of the 1990s can be viewed as a classic example that demonstrates an efficient synthesis among these three tracks. The progression in this historic peace process seems to be taken from an attractive recipe, written in the handbook for peacemaking diplomacy. Track II diplomacy is turned into secret diplomacy that leads to track I diplomacy.

The Oslo Accord was initiated through secret track II meetings between a small group of Israeli academics and several low ranking officials from the PLO. The initiative was developed outside of the stagnant official negotiations in Washington that were being conducted at the same time, following the Madrid conference in 1991.[17] It was an unofficial exploration of possibilities for reaching a peace agreement. However, the participants were well connected and had almost a direct channel of communication to the leadership at the highest level. Indeed, almost from the beginning, any progress was reported back to the political leaders from both sides. The feedback that was received indicated the boundaries of any possible compromise to the process participants. As soon as it became clear that the Oslo talks might result in a formal agreement, the Palestinians requested raising the level of the talks. The Israeli team was expanded to include official negotiators, and track II diplomacy turned into secret diplomacy.[18]

The Oslo Accord was formalized with the Declaration of Principles (DOP) in Oslo Norway, in August 1993. It was officially signed in Washington on September 13, 1993, by Israeli Prime Minister Yitzhak Rabin and PLO leader Yasser Arafat. The agreement proposed a framework for the future relations between Israel and the anticipated Palestinian state (although there was not any specific commitment to establish an independent Palestinian state).[19] After the agreement was signed, track I talks became the main channel for negotiations between the two sides, while back channel diplomacy continued to support the process.[20] The intentions were to prepare the ground for the formal negotiations of a permanent agreement, which was planned to begin no later than May 1996.

From a realist point of view, it looked as if one of the main reasons that the political-elite model in the Oslo case worked so effectively, efficiently, and smoothly, was the motivation of the political leadership at the highest level to reach an agreement. It seemed that both leaders, Yitzhak Rabin and Yasser Arafat, needed to conclude a peace agreement for their own political survival. Rabin, the architect of the 1967 war, was elected on the belief that he was the only leader that could conclude an agreement with the Palestinians without endangering the security of Israel. However, he was about to disappoint his voters by failing to fulfill his 1992 campaign promise – to deliver an agreement with the Palestinians within six to nine months after the general elections in Israel.[21] Arafat, who was in exile at that time, faced major difficulties in retaining his position as the ultimate leader of the Palestinian people. It looked like he did not have much control over the *Intifada*, the spontaneous uprising of the Palestinian people in the territories. His organization, the PLO, experienced a severe financial crisis which damaged its ability to function.[22] In the meantime, Hamas, the radical Islamist movement, built an impressive chain of charity in the territories and its credibility, popularity, and influence grew rapidly, especially among the younger generation.[23]

Both leaders understood that a drastic change was needed in order to restore their political position. However, the official negotiations in Washington (track I diplomacy) were stalled. The official policy of Israel and the US was no negotiating with the PLO, which was considered to be a terrorist organization. Arafat, from his side, conducted many efforts to sabotage any talks with the Palestinians that he and his organization were not a central part of. The unconventional diplomatic initiative that started in Oslo was a precious opportunity for both leaders.

The nature of the track II process enabled the leaders to explore ideas in a way that could not have been done in the official negotiations in Washington. It was the secret, unofficial and not obligatory talks which enabled them to indirectly explore creative ideas that even contradicted their official policy. The nature of the process was extremely valuable in reaching a breakthrough and sketching the historic draft of Declaration of Principles.[24]

A lot of ink has been spilt to demonstrate that political leaders should not be trusted. Their intentions are not always benevolent, to say the very least, and their ability to bring salvation in a complex situation of social crisis is very limited. Nevertheless, the Oslo peace process, like almost any attempt to promote a solution to the Palestinian-Israeli conflict, has been mainly dependent on the dubious goodwill and talent of political leaders.

The Oslo process did not involve the public in any substantial way. It was almost entirely dependent on political leaders (Rabin and Arafat) who were ambivalent toward the peace process that they initiated, approved, and blessed. Perhaps, secrecy, unconventional methods of back channel diplomacy, and the central part that top leaders played in the accord were the only ways to reach a historic agreement. However, it was not enough to give the peace process a life of its own. The reality was that both sides continued to keep the struggle alive: the Palestinians built up military capacity beyond the level stipulated in the agreement and did not stop the incitement of violence against Israel, while the Israelis continued to expand and strengthen the settlement project.[25]

The public from both sides were not prepared for necessary compromises that a peace process required and to trust the other side in times of expected crises. The lack of social foundations for an effective and reasonable peace process enabled extremists, radicals, and professional spoilers to continue dictating conditions for the rest of the societies. In 1995 Rabin was assassinated by a radical Israeli who probably opposed the Oslo Accord. The ongoing terrorist attacks within Israel, during this time, gave the impression that the new Israeli government, under the leadership of Shimon Peres, was caught in a "blind" race toward an imaginary peace process. It was not clear if the Palestinians were ready for a realistic negotiation and the Israelis were prepared for a reasonable peace process.

The dissonance between the grand peace vision of Peres – "New Middle East" (a prosperous peaceful region) – and the tragic reality on the ground brought a new right-wing government to power in Israel. The new government, under the leadership of Benjamin Netanyahu, advocated a different line of thinking than the Oslo path.

Unfortunately, one crisis led to another until the collapse of the Oslo peace process into the second *Intifada* in 2000. Ironically, every side blamed the other for the failure of an innovative process which was intended to put an end to the Palestinian-Israeli struggle.[26] The questions that remain are: Can we regard the Oslo peace process as a failure? What lessons can be learned from this innovative accord? How to prevent repeating the same mistakes? How can we use the political-elite model in the most beneficial, effective, and efficient way?

Summary

The Oslo Accord is a masterpiece in peacemaking diplomacy. It demonstrates how to use the diplomatic channels of the political-elite model to initiate a revolutionary peace process in a situation that looks most desperate. The failure of the accord to bring peace and stability to the region demonstrates major weaknesses of the political-elite model. It does not involve the people in the peacemaking process and does propose mechanisms to build the foundations of a new social order. The political-elite model cannot sustain a lasting peace by itself alone.

The political-elite model can be very effective in initiating a peace process, supporting it, and concluding agreements between policy makers and leaders. Its back channel modes of communication (track II and secret diplomacy) can be very efficient in dealing with "sensitive" issues that require careful treatment, delicate process, and complete secrecy. The price is that the public is not involved in the peacemaking efforts. Mostly, the people are not prepared to deal with all the necessary consequences that a revolutionary peace process entails.

The preparation of the people for an innovative peace process is critical in situations of intractable conflict, like the Palestinian-Israeli struggle, where ordinary people are in the center of the conflict. Major crises should be expected and careful preparation is required to bypass major obstacles and to move on to the next step.

The Oslo Accord, like many other peacemaking efforts in similar cases of intractable conflict, indicates that as the peace process begins to accelerate, violence tends to increase. One of the reasons is that extremists, radicals, and "professional" spoilers are making all possible efforts to wreck the process and continue dictating conditions to the rest of society. People, on opposing sides, who are prepared to open a new page in their relationships, understand that the only answer to such provocative episodes is to continue promoting the culture of peace by all means. However, they need instruments to cope with expected and unexpected complications. Unfortunately, the political-elite model does not provide effective tools to cope with major crises that threaten to destroy the whole process.

Major bold initiatives in almost every dimension of our life – such as: science, research business, and technology – tend to fail in bringing the expected results, at least in the first attempts. Likewise, most innovative efforts to put an end to the difficult situation of intractable conflict do not succeed in solving the problem. However, these failures are extremely valuable: they help us to better understand the challenge; they increase our knowledge of the complexity of the situation; they give us a better indication about possible solutions to the conflict; and they motivate creative peacemakers to try again with much more carefulness and preparation.[27]

The sophisticated peacemaker, who wishes to get the maximum benefit from the political-elite model and minimize risks and damages, is advised to consider the following:

- To use the various channels of the political-elite model simultaneously.
- To develop trust and good working relationships with the other side.
- To regard the peacemaking process as a joint problem that the opposing leaderships have to solve together.
- To prepare with the other side a joint emergency plan for situations of severe crises.
- To search for creative ways to prepare the people for a revolutionary peace process without damaging the efficiency of the secret and intimate channels that the political-elite model offers.
- To create joint mechanisms for implementing agreements and solving future problems, frictions, and tensions.[28]

The political-elite is a conflict resolution model that, probably, cannot solve the conflict by itself alone. Only superhuman peacemaking leaders on both sides can consider and implement those six critical points simultaneously. The inevitable conclusion is that building the foundations of a peaceful social order requires implementing various peacemaking models, strategies, and approaches simultaneously. The public-assembly model, our next peacemaking model, is designed to involve the people in the peacemaking efforts and to invite peacemaking leaders to appear on the political stage of the Middle East.

7 The public-assembly model

Introduction

There is a broad consensus among analysts that everything has been said and done in regard to the Palestinian-Israeli struggle. This view, which does not leave much room for optimism, is not surprising. Intractable conflict is a severe social crisis. However, in the study of humanities and social sciences it is almost impossible to predict future developments.[1] There are always astonishing and unpredicted developments that could never have been imagined. Indeed, after the Second World War, when the hate between the two sworn enemies France and Germany had reached its peak, who could have imagined that 50 years later they would be among the founders of a European confederation, the European Union.

In the 1970s the most entrenched conflicts in the world were considered to be the struggle in Apartheid South Africa, the "troubles" in Northern Ireland, and the Palestinian-Israeli conflict.[2] It was impossible to forsee that South Africa and Northern Ireland would experience drastic changes, while the Palestinian-Israeli conflict would remain in the same old track of destruction. The expectations of the people, at least in Northen Ireland and Israel, were different than the developments on the ground. The consensus among the people in Northern Ireland was that the American Senator George Mitchell, who was the chairperson of the peace process, was simply wasting his time.[3] In contrast, the Oslo peace process gave a lot of hope to the Israeli people who believed that days of peace were coming to Israelis and Palestinians.

The complexity of protracted social conflicts, which make them so intractable, indicates that there is always room for new ideas. This chapter presents the public-assembly model which is designed to promote the culture of peace and bring new and creative ideas to the consideration of the people in the opposing societies. It is intended to help the public on both sides discover and experience the meaning of a realistic peace process. It adds an important dimension that is missing from almost any substantial peacemaking initiative.

A critical component that is absent from almost every peace process in the Palestinian-Israeli situation is the involvment and participation of the people. The people in Israel and Palestine woke up one morning and heard about the Oslo peace process which intended to open a new page in their joint tragic history. They were not prepared for, or involved in, this important initiative. And without the adequate preparation, it is quite easy for spoilers to sabotage the process and continue to dictate conditions for the rest of the people.

The public-assembly model proposes a mechanism that can close this gap. The model suggests establishing a major Plaestinian-Israeli public assembly. The assembly is a public negotiating congress which intends to prepare the people for a reasonable peace process through provoking a public debate in the opposing societies. This peace-building institution is new in the Palestinian-Israeli experience. However, the vision is loosely based upon the multi-party talks that helped to stabilize, for quite a long time, two desperate situations of intractable conflict: the struggle against the Apartheid regime in South Africa and the "troubles" in Northern Ireland.

The public-assembly model

The public-assembly model is designed to actively involve the people of both sides in the peacemaking process in order to bring it to the point of no return. This model proposes to establish a major Palestinian-Israeli public-assembly – a public negotiating congress. The assembly is a democratic institution in which representatives or delegations are invited to discuss, debate, and negotiate different solutions to the conflict by peaceful means.

Like a democratic congress, the assembly has to reflect the different opinions in the general public and discourage any attempt to achieve political power through violence. Three methods of choosing representatives could give the assembly credibility: (1) holding general elections in the opposing societies specifically for the assembly, (2) inviting the institutions involved in the conflict to send delegations, (3) asking various societal sectors (such as: academia, business, and clergy) to appoint delegates. A firm rule to begin with is that every participant has to commit to stop, or at least to suspend, the violent struggle and condemn any effort to gain political achievements by destructive means.[4]

In general, the main agenda of the public-assembly is to find a solution to the conflict or, at least, to formulate acceptable general principles for a future agreement. Unfortunately, it is likely that the assembly will not be able to achieve this goal. Reaching a peace agreement in a major public-assembly is extremely difficult, as issues that are perceived as existential are at stake. It is hard to imagine that a public-assembly that gives a voice to all opposing opinions, including those of radicals and extremists, will succeed in producing an acceptable agreement. The complexity of the struggle indicates that the chance of reaching a conclusive peace pact is more likely to be achieved in the more intimate process offered by the various channels of the political-elite model.[5] However, the public-assembly's main tasks are to prepare the opposing societies for a reasonable peace process, to create peacemaking coalitions, and to invite visionary leaders to the stage of politics. Therefore, the establishment of this peace building institution is critical for laying the foundations for peaceful relationships between Palestinians and Israelis.

One of the main objectives of the public-assembly is to provoke a public debate over central issues. Public debate and open discussions around "sanctified" controversial matters are necessary for progress. They have the potential to penetrate doubts about entrenched positions and to help people find it worthwhile to consider alternatives that previously were not even taken into account.[6] This is a key element in seeking, searching, understanding, and accepting creative solutions.

Public debate is the spirit of any pluralistic mechanism. It is an instrument that gives a stage to different opinions and engages the population in a critical discussion.[7] The negotiations in the assembly will place on the public agenda obstacles for peace that are considered taboo, such as Jerusalem, borders, and the right of return.[8] Public debate has the potential to change the public's mindset, even without its conscious attention. For example, it can help people to step outside the conventional wisdom that there is no solution to the conflict, by bringing them to consider, evaluate, and debate different potential solutions. In short, a serious public debate helps to connect the people to the peace process and create an atmosphere of hostility toward the continuation of the violence (as defined by the two communities). It is a necessary component in the transformation of an armed struggle into a political contest.

The multi-party talks in South Africa and Northern Ireland

The vision of a major Palestinian-Israeli public assembly – a public negotiating congress – is based loosely on the multi-party talks that helped to create a dramatic change in two other desperate situations of intractable conflict: the struggle against racial segregation in Apartheid South Africa and Northern Ireland during the "troubles." In both cases it was extremely difficult to establish the assemblies. The assemblies collapsed again and again. The talks were frequently stopped and for a long time it looked as though it would be impossible to reach a peace agreement.[9] Moreover, paramilitary groups continued their violent actions. However, the assemblies had important contributions in preparing the people for considering options of reasonable compromises toward the establishment of a peaceful social order.

In South Africa in 1991, 228 delegates representing 19 political parties came together to form the Convention of Democratic South Africa (CODESA) in order to negotiate binding principles for the future constitutional assembly.[10] The CODESA talks, which were designed to form the foundation for a new South Africa, collapsed and reestablished only to collapse again (CODESA2). The Multiparty Negotiating Forum (MPNF) grew out of the failure of the CODESA talks in 1993. Major violent events – such as the massacres in the South African towns of Boipatong and Bisho in 1992 and the assassination of South African Communist Party leader Chris Hanni in 1993 – threatened to derail the whole process. However, these violent events could not stop the peace train from moving forward. At the end of the day they encouraged the two major parties and the top leaders to make extensive efforts to achieve a negotiated settlement for a new South Africa.[11]

In Northern Ireland, the Forum for Peace and Reconciliation was created in 1994; the Northern Ireland Forum followed in 1996; and the Belfast Assembly was established by the Good Friday Agreement of 1998.[12] However, as Senator Mitchell noted, the troubles did not end with the signing of the Good Friday Agreement but with the Omagh bombing. Twenty–nine men, women, and children died as a result of the attack and approximately 220 people were injured.[13]

The Omagh bombing, which happened a couple of months after the signing of the historical Good Friday Agreement, led to an immediate cease-fire for all paramilitary groups operating in Northern Ireland.[14] The people in Northern Ireland, who were tired of fighting, stopped letting radicals, extemists, and spoilers dictate conditions for them. Unfortunately, the current situation in the Palestinian-Israeli case illustrates that any major violent episode has the potential to stop any significant peace initiative. The people in Israel and Palestine are not involved in any substantial peacemaking efforts. It is necessary to create an effective mechanism that can close this gap.

As previously stated, the main function of the public assembly is to involve the people in the peacemaking process and to create an atmosphere of change. Therefore, the successes and failures of public negotiating assemblies are not necessarily measured by their length of their tenure or their ability to come up with a conclusive peace pact. An agreement is likely to be finalized in the channels that the political-elites model proposes. For example, a friendly, informal environment made it easy for British and Irish leaders at the highest level to achieve the historical Good Friday Agreement of 1998, which won the endorsment of most Northern Ireland political parties.[15]

Successful public negotiating assemblies are those that prepare people in the opposing societies for a reasonable peace, neutralize the damaging influence of "professional" spoilers, invite visionary leaders to the stage of politics, and push them to reach an effective and acceptable compromise. It is the formation and collapse of these assemblies that can lead the peace process to the point of no return.

Two fundamental questions remain open: 1. Is the very idea of a establishing a Palestinian-Israeli public-assembly – a major Public Negotiating Congress – a realistic vision or only a wild fantasy? 2. How can we start creating the social conditions to establish the foundations for this peace building institution in a destructive reality that seems to be hopeless?

The mirror image

As strange as it may sound, public-opinion surveys, even after the Gaza crisis at the end of 2008, show that large majorities in the Palestinian and Israeli societies prefer to end the conflict by peaceful means. Of course, "peaceful means" is an elusive concept that has different meanings to different people. However, results of a poll in April 2009 indicate that 74 percent of Palestinians and 78 percent of Israelis are willing to accept a two state solution.[16] Moreover, 77 percent of Israelis and 71 percent of Palestinians find a negotiated peace to be essential and desirable.[17] Nevertheless, the actual behavior of the two people – which constantly contradicts their declarations, aspirations, and best interests – does not necessarily follow the logic of these findings.

The aspirations and hopes of the Israeli public for a peaceful resolution to the conflict is not surprising. The majority of the public in Israel has already demonstrated, over and over again, its desire for a serious and effective peace process. For example, Yitzhak Rabin, Prime Minister during the Oslo period, was elected on the belief that he was the only leader who could bring peace.[18] The apex of Ariel Sharon's popularity was reached after his historical unilateral withdrawal from Gaza.

Ironically, without almost any connection to the chain of crises that followed Sharon's dramatic move, his unilateral withdrawal had contributed substantially to the growing understanding among the Israeli population that promoting a reasonable solution to the conflict is essential for Israel.[19] Tragically, many Israelis still believe that Sharon, whose illness forced him to step out of politics, was the only leader who could bring peace and security to Israel. However, public opinion during a situation of an ongoing conflict can shift quite easily, as it depends on many factors such as the behavior of the other side. Indeed, the Israeli public view is teetering between hope and despair, right, and left.

The ongoing violent attacks inside Israel since the Oslo agreement have contributed to the Israeli view that it is impossible, or at least very dangerous, to make peace with the Palestinians. For example, Israel's security problems contributed to the astonishing defeat of Shimon Peres, a peacemaking visionary, by Benjamin Netanyahu, a right-wing hardliner, in the 1996 general elections. Even in academic circles, intellectuals began to develop a strategy to cope with a situation of ongoing conflict. The conflict-management strategy, which has been developed by scholars from the Bar-Ilan and Hebrew universities, intends to help Israel survive in a situation of an unsolved conflict.[20] Again, the motivation is the perception that the Palestinian society is a failed entity that can produce only terror. Israelis look at the political division in Palestinian society as a piece of evidence that supports this view. It is difficult for Israelis to accept the view that most Palestinians are willing to join a substantial initiative for promoting the resolution of the conflict by peaceful means. The recent events in Gaza (the ongoing rocket attacks on Israeli towns launched by Hamas) demonstrate for Israelis that the language of force is inevitable in this situation. The results are that the 2009 elections in Israel gave substantial political power again to the Israeli right wing.

It is difficult to reconcile a referendum showing that Palestinians prefer peace with the fact that in January 2006 Hamas, the radical Islamist party, was successful in the Palestinian parliamentary elections, taking most seats in the chamber. Part of the explanation for this contradiction is that a majority of Palestinians believe that most Israelis are not interested in peace. In their view, the Jewish-Israeli project equals Zionist Imperialism.[21] Unfortunately, the miserable circumstances contribute to the rise of political radicalism in Palestinian society.

The phenomenon in which each side is convinced that its rival is not interested in peace is labeled the "mirror image."[22] This well-known symptom appears in many similar intractable conflicts. This entrenched idea that there are no human beings who understand the meaning of peace on the other side, helps to escalate the violent cycle. Moreover, it prepares the ground for extremists and "professional" spoilers to shape a policy that is destructive for both sides.

The root of the mirror image, at least in the moderate majority, is ignorance of the other side's difficulties and aspirations. Each side is entrenched in its own position without realizing that its strategy for coping with the difficulties only worsens the situation. Any act of violence, even for self-defense, is understood by the other side as additional proof of the inhumanity of its rival. Senator Mitchell describes this tragic situation in his report of the 2001 Sharm el-Sheik Fact-Finding Committee:

> Despite their long history and close proximity, some Israelis and Palestinians seem not to fully appreciate each other's problems and concerns.

Some Israelis appear not to comprehend the humiliation and frustration that Palestinians must endure every day as a result of living with the continuing effects of occupation, sustained by the presence of Israeli military forces and settlements in their midst, or the determination of the Palestinians to achieve independence and genuine self-determination. Some Palestinians appear not to comprehend the extent to which terrorism creates fear among the Israeli people and undermines their belief in the possibility of coexistence . . . Fear, hate, anger and frustration have risen on both sides. The greatest danger of all is that the culture of peace, nurtured over the previous decade, is being shattered. In its place there is a growing sense of futility and despair, and a growing resort to violence.[23]

Unfortunately, the mirror-image effect prepares the ground for a tragic situation wherein the strategy of violence replaces the culture of peace. This conviction – the entrenched idea that it is impossible to develop peaceful relationships with the other side – has to be broken in order to build the foundations for a peaceful social order. The public-assembly model can be very useful for this task. The model offers a mechanism that can help each side to understand the culture, mentality, fears, and needs of the opponent. The negotiations in the assembly, as difficult as they can be, help to breach the old convention that it is impossible to build peaceful relationships with the other side. The Minds of Peace Experiment – a small-scale Palestinian-Israeli public negotiating assembly – which will be presented and discussed later, demonstrates this important observation.

Peacemaking as a learning process

One of the main motivations to involve the public in the peacemaking process is the broad understanding in each society that it is impossible to defeat the opponent by violent means. The Palestinians understand that they cannot defeat Israel, while most of the Israelis realize that in the long run it will be impossible to stop Palestinian insurgency by militaristic means. However, without a strategy to promote the culture of peace, violence and escalation will probably continue to dominate the situation. The two communities need to see a viable alternative to the violent struggle. A major Palestinian-Israeli public negotiating assembly is designed to transform the violent discourse into a political process.

The assembly functions like a congress for conflict resolution. The various delegations, representing different parts of each population, are invited to introduce and promote their interests and worldviews. The assembly will exclude anyone who wishes to continue the violent struggle and refuse to promote his or her objectives by peaceful means. Therefore, the representatives are compelled to learn how to debate the most important and sensitive issues by peaceful means. This competitive pluralism[24] is a powerful mechanism that helps the opposing factions to learn about the culture and mentality of the other side, and maneuvers them to search for new knowledge and explore creative ideas. The public assembly is designed to replace the current destructive competition, the violent struggle, by peaceful negotiation.[25]

The vitality of the public assembly, in contrast to the secret and intimate processes of back channel diplomacy, depends upon extensive publicity. The public becomes informed about the intention to establish such an institution, and this creates an atmosphere that "something new" is happening. This momentum has the potential to create a positive chain reaction. Every party is stimulated to influence the process and not to be excluded from the center of events. The experiences in Northern Ireland and South Africa show that over time the level of violence is reduced and political parties, which are associated with paramilitary group, tend to join the assembly and commit to follow the rules of the process.[26] However, again, the influence of the different players in the opposing societies can be constructive and destructive on the discussions in the assembly.

It is quite clear that groups that are not interested in peace will try to sabotage the process. Moreover, it is expected that violence, at least in the short run, will increase. Therefore, it is important that the participants in the assembly are willing to commit to suspending the violent struggle and explore possible reactions to major violent episodes that threaten to wreck the whole process. The assembly has to be prepared to face situations of extreme crisis.

The main limitation of the assembly lies in its limited ability, or more precisely inability, to reach a conclusive peace pact. Senator Mitchell constantly complained that the publicity and the scandals that accompanied the multiparty talks in Northern Ireland were major obstacles to reaching a peace agreement.[27] However, these elements engaged the people in the peacemaking efforts and gave the process a life of its own. Ironically, elements that disturbed and prevented the negotiating parties from reaching a peace pact in the assembly, made the process concrete to the people in the streets. At the end of the day, the function of the assembly is to involve the people in the peacemaking process and to pave the way for reaching a conclusive peace pact that can be achieved by the leadership in a more intimate forum.

The vision of establishing a major Palestinian-Israeli public-assembly may sound appealing. The question is: How to start building this peacemaking institution in the difficult circumstances of the Palestinian-Israeli struggle?

Between vision and reality

To establish a major Palestinian-Israeli public-assembly, which invites representatives of the two people to negotiate solutions to their tragic conflict, sounds like a dream. There are major obstacles in almost every possible dimension, from psychological barriers to logistic impediments.[28] Moreover, the idea is not even on the agenda of the public, the leadership, and the international community. The questions are: How to attract attention to this visionary idea? Is it possible to create this peace-building institution? Where do we start?

In Northern Ireland and South Africa, the multi-party assemblies did not spring spontaneously. Their establishment required the application of sophisticated political moves, creative tactics, and political pressure, mainly through the various channels that the political-elite model provides. In Northern Ireland it was external players, the English and Irish governments, who pulled the strings in order to convene the various forms of the all-party talks.[29] In South Africa, it was the intimate relationship between two strong leaders Frederik Willem DeKlerk, the last president of the Apartheid era, and Nelson Mandela, the leader of the black majority, that enabled the formalization of the multi-party negotiating congress (CODESA) and pushed the peace process forward.[30] These diplomatic connections helped bypass major impediments.

In Northern Ireland, one of the main obstacles to establishing the multi-party talks was the Irish Republican Army (IRA), which refused to decommission itself and stop the violent struggle. In order to bypass this barrier, the British and the Irish governments insisted on democratic elections to a multi-party assembly.[31] However, democratic elections to a multi-party congress were the nightmare of the whites in South Africa. The people in the Apartheid government were convinced that democratic elections to a constitutional assembly that would determine the fate of South Africa, would lead to a substantial black majority in the chamber. They preferred a constitutional convention composed of representatives from all existing political institutions. However, this kind of convention would never be able to reflect the diversity of the South African population (20 million blacks versus 5 million whites). The non-white parties saw in this proposal a cheap trick, a way to maintain a softer version of Apartheid. Only diplomatic contacts between leaders from both sides at the highest level could conclude a sophisticated compromise to the satisfaction of both sides.[32]

In the Palestinian-Israeli case, the establishment of a major public assembly is going to be extremely difficult. We have not seen visionary peacemaking leaders who understand the importance of involving the people in a peacemaking process emerge in Middle-Eastern politics. The international community does not show signs of making serious efforts to promote the idea of a Palestinian-Israeli public assembly.[33] Therefore, it is worth considering that a major public assembly – a public negotiating congress – will emerge from the grassroots level.

The idea is to conduct simulations of a major Palestinian-Israeli public assembly in various places around the world and in Israel/Palestine. These simulations, which I am labeling the "Minds of Peace Experiment," have multiple functions: demonstrating the peacemaking power of a major public negotiating congress, helping to evaluate its potential outcomes, and building public pressure for a potential accord.

The Minds of Peace Experiment

The Minds of Peace Experiment is a simulation of a major Palestinian-Israeli public negotiating congress. The exercise is not only a simulation. It is a small public negotiating assembly that invites five Israelis to meet five Palestinians in order to negotiate solutions to their tragic struggle.[34] The assembly is co-chaired by Palestinian and Israeli moderators.[35]

The formal negotiations are conducted in front of an audience. At the end of each formal session, the audience is invited to ask questions, comment, and make suggestions. The practical meaning is that the debate is conducted on three levels: between the delegations, within each delegation, and between the delegations and the audience.

The general assignment of the assembly is to reach a peace agreement in five formal sessions. As a preliminary stage the delegations are requested to conclude an agreement on confidence building measures and on the suspension of the violent struggle. This is a necessary stage that the assembly has to reach before the negotiations on a conclusive peace pact begin. The purpose of the preliminary stage is to create commitment to the process, to build trust between the participants and to establish an atmosphere of peacemaking. However, it is a very difficult stage. One of the reasons is that "violent struggle" has different meanings for Palestinians and Israelis. For example, part of the Palestinians views the check points in the West Bank as a violent reality while part of the Israeli population regards it as a self-defense necessity. The meaning of the term "violent struggle" has to be negotiated at the beginning of the public assembly and to be translated into practical measures.[36]

There are two ground rules for the discussion. The first is not to demean each other. The second is not to enter into a historical debate upon the origin of the conflict and past evils. The delegations are instructed to focus upon improving the present situation, to visualize a peaceful future, to come up with language that works for both parties, and to make demands by peaceful means.[37]

The ground rules are designed to make the discussions efficient and constructive. However, it is likely that the assembly will not be able to reach a conclusive peace agreement in the formal negotiations because the issues at stake are too complicated and sensitive. In addition, the delegations are not homogeneous i.e. each one of the participants have its own political view. In order to make the negotiations in the assembly effective, the two delegations are encouraged to engage in informal settings, such as: secret negotiations and Track-II diplomacy.[38] They are instructed and motivated by the mediators to come prepared to the formal settings in the assembly.

The success of the "Minds of Peace Experiment" is not necessarily measured by its ability to produce a final peace pact. The main purpose of the "Minds of Peace Experiment" is to provoke a public debate in the local community, to demonstrate the complexity of the situation, to denounce violence, and to explore what ordinary people can do in order to promote peace.[39]

The experiments

We conducted the "Minds of Peace Experiment" nine times: six times in the United States and three times in Israel/Palestine. The rounds in the United States were conducted in different universities: University of Missouri-St. Louis (twice), Wayne State University, University of California-Irvine, University of Michigan-Ann Arbor, and University of California Los Angeles. The Middle East rounds were conducted in the Everest Hotel in Beit Jala (near Jerusalem).[40] The Palestinian and the Israeli delegations in the various rounds were heterogeneous in regard to substantial parameters, such as: political view, gender, age, education, and occupation.

The experiment has proven to be a fascinating laboratory for people-to-people diplomacy and people-to-people negotiation. For example, the experiment succeeded in demonstrating the complexity of the situation, it showed that there are major objective problems that have to be discussed and solved (not everything is psychology), it illustrated how to effectively combine two competitive methods of negotiation: "bargaining" and "problem solving", it cemented the idea that there are peace lovers on both sides who wish to end this conflict by peaceful means, and it helped to create commitment to learn the language of peace in extremely difficult circumstances. Ironically, in many sessions it was the hardliners who led their delegation toward a compromise that they usually objected to and rejected in the past. We learned that not only professional politicians like Sadat and Sharon can change their political strategy dramatically.

It is not surprising that the negotiating processes and their outcomes were different each time. People are different, they hold diverse worldviews, and their interactions depend upon many variables and factors. Each round emphasized different aspects of the conflict. For example, a central issue in the Detroit round (Wayne State University) was the dispute over the right of the Palestinian refugees to go back to Israel ("the right of return"); while the central motif in the first round in the Middle East (Israel/Palestine) was dismantling check points versus security.

Each negotiating process was dominated by different characteristics of the interactions between Israelis and Palestinians, for example: asymmetrical conflict (Israel has a better bargaining position), tiredness from the struggle and eagerness to find a peaceful resolution, lack of trust, stereotypes and initial beliefs, and the need for creative solutions to complicated problems. No doubt that a comprehensive study, which the author of this book is conducting in another place, is needed in order to fully analyze and evaluate the experiments and the lessons they enfold to policy makers, ordinary people, and professional negotiators. Ironically, the most important issue for our purpose here – possibilities for establishing a major Palestinian-Israeli public negotiating congress – can be found in the similarities between nine small public negotiating assemblies that were so different from one another.

Beyond almost any expectations the assemblies did not collapse. Moreover, each one of them succeeded in producing at least one agreement.[41] This result was especially noticeable in the first round in Israel/Palestine. Most of the Palestinians, who were religious Muslims, fasted during the whole negotiating process because of the Ramadan (the Islamic month of fasting). This difficulty did not disturb their enthusiasm to negotiate peace and the two delegations, despite major differences in worldviews, succeeded in concluding two agreements.[42] As impressive as it may be, this was not the most important achievement of the assembly.

The most important result of the Minds of Peace is not the agreements that each assembly achieved. The critical issue is hidden in a side effect that each assembly created – peace coalitions. The nine rounds of the Minds of Peace Experiment showed clearly the potential of small public negotiating assemblies to create grassroots peace coalitions. The coalitions, which are built from the negotiators and the audience, manifested in various ways, such as: activism – peacemaking initiatives grew out of the assemblies (including the Minds of Peace Organization which has been supported by members of the St. Louis community); commitment – Palestinians and Israelis committed to continue and develop the initiative; interest – people in the audience that do not have any stake in the conflict have expressed sincere wishes to continue and develop the initiative; cohesion – most of the experiments in the Diaspora helped to strengthen the connections between the different local communities: Jews, Muslims, and Christians.

The glue that connects the peace coalitions that each assembly created is not necessarily love or altruistic motivations, but a deep understanding of the importance of negotiation, debate, and critical discussion. These are critical elements for building the foundations of a peaceful social order. The questions are: How to transform this peacemaking effect – the ability of small public negotiating assemblies to create peace coalitions – into a mass movement? How to attract substantial attention to the initiative? How to create a massive domestic and international pressure to establish a major Palestinian-Israeli Public Negotiating Congress?

Obstacles and political barriers

Conducting public negotiating assemblies in different locations around Israel and the disputed territories on a regular basis is an essential task. It can demonstrate the peacemaking power of public negotiations and develop momentum for potential accord. Unfortunately, the current political situation does not permit the implementation of this peacemaking program. There is no free movement between Israel and the Palestinian territories for most of the local inhabitants. In other words, Israelis cannot visit the West Bank without special permission and, vice versa, Palestinians cannot enter Israel without the approval of the authorities.

There are very few social spaces where Israelis and Palestinians can meet without asking permission from governmental authorities. Indeed, as previously noted, the "Minds of Peace Experiment" was conducted three times in Beit Jala (near Jerusalem and Beit Lechem), one of the few places that Israelis and Palestinians from the West Bank can meet without too many complications.

True, the audience is growing larger from one assembly to the next. However, many of the people in the audience are peace activists that already engage in different kinds of dialogue groups. Moreover, Israelis are afraid to travel to Beit Jala (which is located about 20 minutes from Jerusalem) and there are logistical and political difficulties that prevent Palestinians from attending the assembly. How do we bypass the infinite problems and bring the negotiations to every house in Israel and the Palestinian territories?

We continue to struggle with growing the movement beyond the local level. Attracting local and international media coverage and increasing political support among the Israeli people and the Palestinian public to the Minds of Peace initiative and its goals is a challenge. To cope with some of the difficulties we recently began to employ various tools that modern information technology has to offer: live webcasting the following experiments, utilizing the web to announce meetings, posting blogs, publishing peace agreements, introducing the initiative to different groups, recruiting peace activists to spread the word, building networks of peacemaking coalitions, and so on.

No doubt that there are many obstacles and difficulties in creating a mass movement that can prepare the ground for the establishment of a major public negotiating congress. However, we should bear in mind that creating change-building institutions, such as the Civil Rights Movement in the United States and the multi-party talks in Northern Ireland and South Africa did not happen in one day. The road to create these peacemaking projects was paved with many difficulties and obstacles.

Summary

The missing component in almost any substantial peacemaking initiative in the Palestinian-Israeli case was the participation, preparation, and involvement of the people in the process. The public-assembly model proposes to establish a major Palestinian-Israeli public negotiating congress in order to fill this gap. The assembly invites representatives of the opposing societies to discuss, debate, and negotiate solutions to their tragic conflict. The dialogue, discussions, and negotiations in the assembly intend to provoke a public debate within each society. This peacemaking process is necessary to build the foundations of a peaceful social order.

Despite the results of the Minds of Peace Experiment (a small-scale public negotiating assembly), it is quite clear that it will be extremely difficult for a major public negotiating assembly to conclude a conclusive peace pact. Indeed, the multi-party talks in Northern Ireland and South Africa were launched from one crisis to another, violence continued during the talks, and the negotiators had a difficult time finalizing the process.

The Oslo peace process indicates that secrecy and the intimate features of back channel diplomacy are sometimes necessary to reach a breakthrough. The delicate channels of the political-elite model (track II and secret diplomacy) provide effective tools for reaching agreements in situations of intractable conflicts when sensitive issues, which are perceived as existential by the different parties, are at stake. The participants in the secret engagement of the Oslo Accord succeeded in concluding an agreement while the official talks in Washington were stalled. One of the main functions of the public-assembly is to prepare the people to accept innovative and historic agreements. This was a critical element that was missing from the Oslo peace process.

The political-elite and the public-assembly are two competitive conflict-resolution models that should be implemented simultaneously.[43] The political-elite model provides efficient channels for leaders to begin, support, and finalize a peace process. The public-assembly model intends to involve the people in the peacemaking process, prepare the public to accept necessary compromises, and invite visionary leaders to the stage of politics.

In the Palestinian-Israeli struggle, the people who are in the center of the conflict suffer the most. It is their responsibility to create the conditions for a revolutionary peace process, especially when the leadership does not present a strategy to promote the culture of peace. The pro-negotiating elements in the opposing societies need to join forces in order to create a change by peaceful means. One of the mechanisms to do so is to organize a mass movement that supports and promotes the idea of establishing a major public negotiating congress.

An effective public negotiating congress is a democratic institution that transmits credibility, commitment to a peaceful dialogue, and determination to peacefully resolve the conflict. Lessons from the multi-party talks in Northern Ireland and South-Africa, and the Minds of Peace Experiment are useful in building a vision of a major Palestinian-Israeli public negotiating assembly which is subject to the following recommendations:

- The public-assembly should reflect the diversity of opinions within each society.
- The discussions in the public-assembly should be co-chaired by an Israeli and a Palestinian representative.
- The public-assembly should denounce violence through the following steps:

  1. The meaning of violence should be discussed, negotiated and decided at the beginning of the talks.
  2. Every participant has to commit to principles of negotiation by peaceful means, as decided by the assembly.
  3. The members of the assembly should commit to continue the process even in situations of crises and destructive internal and external events.
  4. The assembly should decide on possible reactions to violent episodes that could threaten to destroy the whole process.

- The members of the assembly should negotiate possible solutions to the conflict.
- The assembly should come up with practical programs to implement and materialize solutions.
- The assembly should recommend substantial political and social moves that can promote the culture of peace.
- The assembly should demand from the leadership of the opposing societies to initiate peacemaking and peace building policy.

- The assembly should ask the international community for help in promoting a peaceful resolution of the conflict.

The multi-party negotiations in Northern Ireland and South Africa played a critical role in preparing the people for a peaceful resolution of the conflict. The Minds of Peace Experiment demonstrates the peacemaking power of a major potential public negotiating congress in the Middle East. The assembly involves the people in the peacemaking process and helps them examine the situation from different angles of vision. This is a key element in fighting entrenched conventions, discovering new vistas and building a constructive change.[44] The question is: Is the assembly supposed to function only in times of ongoing conflict or should it play an important role also in days of peace?

The fate of the Israelis and Palestinians is intertwined. It is a close contact under high pressure that encompassed almost every aspect of social life, from geographical contact to emotional attachment.[45] True, the consensus solution is divorce – two states for the two people. However, a complete divorce is impossible. The two societies will need a joint mechanism to solve future disputes. In an effective peace process the public negotiating assembly can transform into a joint congress for resolving future frictions between the two entities, and coordinating joint enterprises.

A joint congress to separate Palestinian and Israeli independent entities is a proto-federal institution.[46] A federal engagement of Palestinian and Israeli entities sounds like a vision that cannot even be imaginable at this stage. However, federalism is not only a structure. It is also a process. In these difficult circumstances, I suggest looking at federalism as a discovery process, a process where the two opposing societies learn how to peacefully share their joint destiny. The public-assembly model, the proposal to build a major public negotiating congress, offers a mechanism to begin this kind of peace-building process.

Summary and conclusion

This book focuses upon a common tragic phenomenon in the conduct of human affairs: "intractable conflict", or protracted and violent social strife. I propose to examine the problem from a fresh perspective. Instead of hunting for the best, just, and ultimate solutions, I introduce certain general basic conditions that have the potential to transform a situation of destructive conflict into a more peaceful social order.

As a student of the social sciences, I am aware that introducing the "ultimate" answers to complex social problems is a largely impossible task. Indeed, much has been written about social reformers, professional analysts, and policy makers who have suggested "definitive" solutions to complicated problems which themselves may still not yet be fully comprehended by human intelligence. As history shows, a methodology ignoring basic human limitations often causes more harm than benefit.[1] Nevertheless, instead, social scientists can use their expertise in many different beneficial ways.

Researchers of social affairs are able to use their knowledge and experience to point out processes, tendencies, and social conditions that have the greatest potential to minimize suffering and open opportunities to build the foundations for a beneficial social order. It is also a moral obligation for scholars to provide general advice and recommendations that can help lead the combatant factions to discover, by themselves, the road to peace, prosperity, and happiness. Such is the primary challenge of this book.

The central question that the book struggles with is: How to build the foundations for an effective peace process in the Palestinian-Israeli struggle?

The book presents four models of peacemaking. Each of these models, coping with the challenge from a different perspective, therefore provides a different answer:

- The strong-leader model – proposes drastic initiatives carried out by visionary leaders.

- The social-reformer model – offers domestic reforms within each of the opposing societies.
- The political-elite model – suggests interactions between political elites through traditional diplomatic channels.
- The public-assembly model – encourages the creation of a major Palestinian-Israeli public negotiating congress.

Each of these models contains valuable lessons for the peacemaking efforts in the Middle East. No one of them can sustain an effective peace process by itself alone. There is a need to create a peacemaking configuration that implements and integrates insights from the four models and other sources.

The strong-leader model posits that in a desperate situation of protracted social conflict, any improvement of the situation depends on drastic measures taken by a strong political leader. No doubt, innovative initiatives of strong political leaders are necessary to create a momentum for progress. However, our two examples, Sadat's diplomatic offensive in 1977 and Sharon's uni-lateral withdrawal in 2005, show that dramatic initiatives of strong political leaders are not enough to build the foundations of an effective peace pro-cess. Drastic moves of political leaders can create a momentum for negotia-tions (Sadat's case) and it can lead to catastrophic results (Sharon's case). The success and failure of drastic political, diplomatic, or militaristic moves depends upon multidimensional factors that even the strongest leader cannot even begin to imagine or consider, much less actually control. Moreover, to wait until a skilful visionary leader will emerge onto the stage of politics to bring salvation is a dangerous and costly utopia.

The social-reformer model posits that domestic reforms within the oppos-ing societies are necessary to build the foundations of a new social order. The collapse of the Palestinian authority in 2007 drives home that very point. This tragic event clearly demonstrates how without appropriate foun-dations of a well-functioning social order (rules and institutions) any transi-tional period in a fragile situation can easily deteriorate into social collapse, chaos, and domestic violence. The model introduces necessary domestic maneuvers and procedures that should accompany any peace process. These domestic political and social actions are intended to help each society to cope with harmful side effects of any peace process, such as an increase in violent episodes carried out by the enemies of the process.

The recommendations of the social-reformer model intend to improve the socio-political conditions within the opposing societies. These neces-sary measures can greatly reduce the impact of extremists and create new opportunities for peacemaking. But the main disadvantage remains that the model does not offer direct guidelines for building peaceful relation-ships between the two people. Unfortunately, peacemaking interactions and negotiations do not spring spontaneously out of domestic reforms. Nevertheless, the model helps to insure that if a peace process collapses the consequences are not going to be as catastrophic as in the past. The two sides will be able to recover more easily and to go back to the negotiating table to conclude agreements much faster.

The political-elite model posits that the interactions between political-elites and political leaders of both sides are necessary to resolve conflicts. The model proposes efficient diplomatic channels that can help elites to explore, discover, and examine new creative ideas, and conclude agreements that address the fears and needs of the opposing societies.

History shows that interaction between a wide circle of political elites is, perhaps, the only way to begin a peace process, support it, and conclude agreements. The main disadvantage of the political-elite model is that it does not involve the public in the peacemaking process and create the necessary socio-political environment to implement agreements. To put it differently, there is a substantial gap between the achievements that elites can reach in the intimate diplomatic channels of the model and the readiness of the people to accept new creative and innovative solutions. The Oslo peace process is an archetypical example that demonstrates the advantages and disadvantages of the political-elite model.

The public-assembly model is designed to involve the people in the peacemaking efforts and give the process a life of its own. The model proposes to establish a major Palestinian-Israeli public negotiating congress. The congress is a peacemaking and peace-building institution that intends to transform the violent dialogue into a political discourse, constructed to provide a political voice to the different elements in the opposing societies that are willing to commit to non-violent principles of negotiations.[2]

The main advantages of such a congress are: providing a political alternative to the violent struggle; provoking a public debate in the opposing societies; demonstrating that there are peace lovers in the opposing societies; creating peace coalitions; and discouraging violence. Its main limitations are: major difficulties in concluding agreements – an obstacle that can lead to frustration and despair; public negotiating congresses tend to collapse again and again.

The vision of establishing a major Palestinian-Israeli public negotiating congress is loosely based upon the all-party negotiations in Northern Ireland during the "troubles" and the multi-party talks that help to create a remarkable political transformation in Apartheid South Africa. The Minds of Peace Experiment demonstrates the importance of negotiations on multiple levels and shows that a major congress can grow from the grassroots level.

Almost any peacemaking process that succeeded in creating an effective change in a situation of intractable conflict incorporated many elements in multiple dimensions. Often enough, it is difficult to identify the dominant element that led to a turning point in the struggle. Usually, it is a combination of multiple efforts in various dimensions that create a momentum for a positive change.[3]

There can be no doubt that the multi-party talks in South Africa and the all-party negotiations in Northern Ireland during the 1990s took a central role in the peacemaking process. However, it is clear that many other elements enabled the political transformation in these two situations of intractable conflict. For example, in both cases we clearly identify dramatic actions of strong political leaders that succeeded in pushing the train of peace forward.

An important milestone in the transition of South Africa was the release of Nelson Mandela from jail in 1990, by the last president of the Apartheid system, Frederik Willem de Klerk. De Klerk was aware of the dramatic impact that the release of the mythical leader from jail might create and its positive and negative implications:

> September of 1989 seems to have marked the culmination of De Klerk's evolutionary conversion – the moment when he made the decision in his own mind to release Mandela and begin negotiating with the ANC. Thereafter, it was only a matter of bringing his party along with him, and of deciding when and how to do it. How to manage the release was especially problematic. There were fears of an uncontrollable emotional surge in the black community when this messianic figure emerged from his long entombment; the government was haunted by visions of the mass demonstrations that had followed the Ayatollah Khomeini's return to Teheran in 1979 and overwhelmed the regime of Shah Reza Pahlavi.[4]

In Northern Ireland, a dramatic action of the British Secretary of State, Mo Mowlam, in January 1998, saved the all-party negotiations from collapsing after a major crisis. The bold Secretary of State went to Maze prison to meet personally with prisoners and to ask their support for the continuation of the talks: "the secretary of state for Northern Ireland, one of the British government's highest-ranking officials, seeking a meeting with one hundred and thirty men who had been convicted, by British courts, of murder, bombing and other serious crimes." This was a significant event because "prisoners play an important role in the politics of Northern Ireland. They are seen by some in their communities as heroes who fought to defend a way of life and an oppressed people. Their views are of special significance to the political parties associated with paramilitary organizations." Mo Mowlam, who "took the biggest gamble of her career," succeeded in ensuring the continuation of the talks. The headlines on the day after Mo's visit proclaimed: "'She did it! Gamble pays off for "Mighty Mo."' 'Full credit to Mo Mowlam.' 'Mowlam's Maze visit ensures talks will continue.' The prisoners agreed to continue their support for the talks, and the cease-fire by the main loyalist paramilitary organizations would remain intact. Praise and criticism of Mo aside, the fact remained that, with a combination of skill and daring, she had kept the process intact."[5]

Again, the questions are: How to build the foundations of an effective peacemaking process in the Palestinian-Israeli situation? How to structure a multifaceted approach to peacemaking? How to involve the people in the peacemaking efforts, how to invite visionary peacemaking leaders to the stage of Middle East politics and how to incorporate many other necessary elements that can lead to a peacemaking revolution?

A revolutionary peacemaking process

An intractable conflict is a severe crisis that affects almost any aspect of life in the opposing societies. In order to break the chain of destruction a revolutionary peacemaking process is required. However, not every revolutionary process succeeded in creating a change in the direction of peace. There are peacemaking initiatives that succeeded in creating a momentum for positive transition and resolution and there are innovative peacemaking efforts that failed to fulfill this difficult endeavor. The conventional wisdom is that the American civil rights struggle around the 1960s and the multi-party talks in Northern Ireland and South Africa during the 1990s succeeded in creating a positive revolutionary change;[6] while, the Oslo peace process of the 1990s, the most significant peacemaking process in the Palestinian-Israeli conflict, ended with frustration, despair, and renewed violent struggle. The questions are: Which elements are needed to create a beneficial peacemaking revolution in situations of protracted social conflicts? How to make sure that the transition and transformation is progressing in a constructive direction?[7] How to replace the chain of destruction with an effective peacemaking and peace-building process that has a life of its own?

The models and the case studies presented in this book emphasize three critical elements that are necessary to create a revolutionary peacemaking process in the Palestinian-Israeli case: peacemaking visionary leaders, involvement of the people in the peacemaking efforts, and peacemaking institutions. These elements are intertwined: visionary leaders need public support to create a peacemaking change;[8] people that are involved in the peacemaking efforts invite visionary leaders to the stage of politics and demand peacemaking policy;[9] peacemaking institutions are the glue that connects visionary leaders and ordinary people.

Peacemaking institutions are critical elements that can animate this whole revolutionary structure in the Palestinian-Israeli case. Effective peacemaking institutions involve the public from both sides in the peacemaking process; create peace coalitions and promote innovative revolutionary ideas; provide necessary conditions for visionary leaders to rise; prepare the people for a new social order; and keep the revolution alive in times of drawbacks, crises, and despair.

A major Palestinian-Israeli public negotiating congress is a peacemaking institution. The all-party talks in Northern Ireland, the multi-party talks in South Africa and the Minds of Peace Experiments indicate that the congress provides a political alternative to violent struggle. Moreover, the negotiations in the congress can support and encourage domestic reforms in the opposing societies that are so necessary to stabilize any revolutionary structure (visionary leaders, public involvement, and peacemaking institutions).[10]

A public negotiating congress can be a basis for cooperation in the transitional period and in a post-conflict era. The congress can transform into a proto-federal mechanism that can help to solve future disputes and coordinate joint activities. The congress can be a symbol that reminds each one in the opposing societies of the cost of returning to the violent struggle.[11]

No doubt, there are many obstacles and difficulties in preparing the ground for the establishment of a major Palestinian-Israeli public negotiating congress. However, we should bear in mind that creating effective peacemaking institutions, such as the multi-party talks in South Africa and Northern Ireland, did not happen all in one day. The road to create these peacemaking projects was paved with many difficulties and obstacles. The question is: Where and how do we start?

Conclusion

The Palestinian-Israeli struggle is an archetypical example of an intractable conflict progressing from one crisis to another. In order to create an effective change in this desperate situation a revolutionary peacemaking process is required. This work posits that a multifaceted approach to peacemaking has the greatest potential to create the conditions for an effective peace process.

The philosopher Karl Popper noted that a vision and a political program are needed to construct a decent, peaceful, social order. However, the implementation should be in small steps, subject to checks and balances. In our context, implementing the idea of a multifaceted approach to peacemaking needs to begin wherever the circumstances permit. Unfortunately, the Palestinian-Israeli conflict invites very few opportunities for effective peacemaking initiatives.

Palestinian society is divided. The division is not only geographic but also political. After a tragic civil war, which began in 2006, Gaza is controlled by Hamas, a radical Islamic movement, while the West Bank is under the administrative authority of the PLO, a secular nationalist movement. Each of the opposing leaderships is committed to promoting a different ideology. The official position of Hamas in Gaza is to establish an Islamic autocracy and wage an uncompromising holy war against Israel.[12] The leadership of the PLO in the West Bank gives the impression of making efforts to build the foundations of an independent democratic Palestinian state that could peacefully live side by side with Israel.[13]

The division in Palestinian society illustrates that promoting peace and stability in the region requires the implementation of a dual strategy: reducing the level of violence in the Gaza-Israeli case (conflict-management approach) and creating an effective peace process through negotiations on multiple levels in the West Bank–Israeli situation (conflict-resolution approach). True, the Palestinian people in the two separate entities (Gaza and the West Bank) wish to be united. Moreover, the political situation in one entity has substantial influence upon the atmosphere in the other. However, these are exactly the reasons that it is critical to create an atmosphere of hope in the West Bank that could influence the people in Gaza and not vice versa. Drastic peace-building measures in the Israeli-West Bank situation is very important to curtail escalation of frustration and despair in Gaza.[14]

To create a momentum for an effective peacemaking process, extensive negotiations on multiple levels in the West Bank-Israeli situation should take the first priority. The meaning is to create opportunities for leaders to negotiate solutions to the conflict through the diplomatic channels of the political-elite model and to establish a major Palestinian-Israeli public negotiating congress that can involve the people in the peacemaking efforts. Track II diplomacy and the Minds of Peace Experiment are two complementary channels of communication that can start such an ambitious peacemaking project.

Track II diplomacy, the informal channel of the political-elite model, is a sort of intimate research and exploration between political elites of both sides. The Minds of Peace Experiment is a small-scale public negotiating congress. The first intends to explore creative ideas and reach compromises that can lead to negotiations and agreements between policy makers and political leaders. The second intends to demonstrate the peacemaking potential of a public negotiating congress and create local and international support for its establishment.

These two modes of interactions – track II diplomacy and the Minds of Peace Experiment – have the potential to begin an effective peace process. A multifaceted approach to peacemaking is needed to help the opposing communities discover the road to perpetual peace.

Notes

Note: All URLs live at the time of printing.

Introduction

1 For further discussion of the nature of complex phenomenon, see Hayek (1967).
2 Compare to Inbar (2006) and Landau (2006, 268).
3 Some supporters of the conflict-resolution camp argue that the lack of negotiations between Israel and Hamas, especially in 2007–08, paved the way for the tragic escalation at the beginning of 2009. A similar complication occurred in Northern Ireland. In August 1994, the IRA had declared a cease-fire in expectation that inclusive negotiations would begin immediately. However, the British leadership refused to include the political parties associated with paramilitary groups in the negotiations. Eighteen months later, when no negotiations were in sight, the IRA renewed the violent struggle (Mitchell, 1999, 40–41).
4 See, for example, Inbar (2006).
5 See Hayek (1967).
6 Compare to Landau (2006) and Inbar (2006).
7 See, for example, Banks (1984, 20) and Fisher (1997, 1–2).
8 See, for example, Kelman (1996, 99).
9 Compare to Wantchekon (2004) and Huntington ([1968] 2006, xiii).
10 For a further discussion, see Handelman (2006).
11 See, for example, Aronson (1990).
12 Today, Gaza is controlled by the radical Islamic movement Hamas and the West Bank is administrated by the secular party PLO. For a comprehensive account of the roots of the political struggle within Palestinian society see Abu-Amr (1993).
13 See Huntington ([1968] 2006).
14 For a further discussion see, for example, Agha *et al.* (2004).
15 See, for example, Kelman (1997).

1 Intractable conflict as a complex phenomenon

1 For further discussion of the nature of the complex phenomena, see Hayek (1967).
2 I do not intend to pass any moral judgment on Sharon's political and militaristic

moves. My intention here is to simply demonstrate the phenomenon of unintended consequences. I will continue the discussion on Sharon's unilateral initiatives and their practical implications in Chapter 4: The strong-leader model.

3 Freud ([1933] 1968).

4 Freud ([1933] 1968, 95): "Better it were to tackle each successive crisis with means that we have already to our hands."

5 Identification between human beings as a peacemaking mechanism has already appeared in the writing of Niccolo Machiavelli (about 400 years before Freud). Machiavelli dreamed about the unification of the Italian people, who were constantly engaged in civil wars and class struggle (people, nobles, and the army). Machiavelli in his well-known political pamphlet *The Prince* reminded the fighting factions that they were all descendents of the founders of the great Roman Empire. By appealing to their nationalism, Machiavelli tried to emphasize the common origin of the fighting factions and evoke positive sentiments between them. I will discuss Machiavelli's methods of peacemaking in more detail in Chapter 4: The strong-leader model.

6 Freud ([1933] 1968, 94)

7 Freud ([1933] 1968, 86). Machiavelli (1979a, 108) points out that principalities suffer from instability because of a similar reason – an inevitable tension between the common people and the nobles: "the former wishing not to be oppressed and the latter wishing to oppress."

8 Popper ([1945] 1947, 108) noted that Marx's exaggeration that "all history is history of class struggle" was taken too seriously by some of Marx's followers.

9 Compare to Popper ([1945] 1947, 125–26).

10 For an interesting discussion, analysis, and criticism of Marx's theory of social change, see Popper ([1945] 1947, 124–26), who noted that: "According to Marx, every particular social system must destroy itself, simply because it must create the forces which produce the next historical period."

11 See Francis Fukuyama's foreword to the new edition of Huntington ([1968] 2006).

12 Marxist theory and developing theories focus on different stages of development. Marx speaks about the economic forces that will bring about the destruction of Capitalism. Developing theories concentrate on economic progress as a power that can produce a new era in backward societies. These two kinds of theories are not necessarily in contradiction.

13 Compare to Huntington ([1968] 2006, 6):

> Throughout the 1950s the prevailing assumption of American policy was that economic development – the elimination of poverty, disease, illiteracy – was necessary for political development and political stability. In American thinking the causal chain was: economic assistance promotes economic development, economic development promotes political stability. This dogma was codified into legislation and, perhaps more importantly, it was ingrained in the thinking of officials in AID and other agencies concerned with the foreign assistance programs.

14 Huntington ([1968] 2006, 6):

> India was one of the poorest countries in the world in the 1950s and had only a modest rate of economic growth. Yet through the Congress Party it

achieved a high degree of political stability. Per capita incomes in Argentina and Venezuela were perhaps ten times that in India, and Venezuela had a phenomenal rate of economic growth. Yet for both countries stability remained an elusive goal.

15 A description and personal impression of the political and economic situation of the Palestinian town Ramallah can be viewed at: http://www.ynetnews.com/articles/0,7340,L-3820473,00.html.
16 See, for example, Mitchell (1999).
17 Compare to Huntington ([1968] 2006, 6):

> For in fact, economic development and political stability are two independent goals and progress toward one has no necessary connection with progress toward the other. In some instances programs of economic development may promote political stability; in other instances they may seriously undermine such stability.

18 Huntington (1993, 22): "It is my hypothesis that the fundamental source of conflicts in this new world will not be primarily ideological or primarily economic. The great divisions among humankind and the dominating source of conflict will be cultural."
19 Huntington (1993, 23).
20 Huntington (1993, 23 – 24): "A civilization is a cultural entity . . . A civilization is thus the highest cultural grouping of people and the broadest level of cultural identity people have short of that which distinguishes humans from other species."
21 In general, the goal of the Muslim brotherhood, the organization that created Hamas from its own ranks, is to create a pan-Islamic state as closely as possible to the model that was suggested by Prophet Muhammad and his Companions. For a further discussion on the ideological struggle in the Palestinian society, see Abu-Amr (1993, 8–13).
22 Huntington (1993, 38) pointed out that conflict and violence could occur within each civilization. However, in this case it is not clear whether the Palestinian people belong to an Arab civilization or to an Islamic one. Moreover, it is hard to forget that part of the Palestinian community is Christian.
23 Freud ([1933] 1968, 97):

> On the psychological side two of the most important phenomena of culture are, firstly, a strengthening of the intellect, which tends to master our instinctive life, and, secondly, an introversion of the aggressive impulse, with all its consequent benefits and perils.

24 Popper ([1945] 1947, 93) distinguishes between Marx's views and the interpretation of Marx by his followers:

> . . . the Vulgar Marxist is sometimes concerned with the problem of reconciling the claims of Marx with those of Freud and Adler; and if he does not choose one or other of them, he may perhaps decide that hunger, love and lust for power are the Three Great Hidden Motives of Human Nature brought to light by Marx, Freud and Adler, the Three Great Makers of the modern man's philosophy.

25 For example, major violent episodes on almost a regular basis accompanied the Oslo peace process in the Middle East, the multiparty talks in South Africa and the all party talks in Northern Ireland. I will analyze this phenomenon and its implications in Chapters 5, 6, and 7.

26 The "mirror image" was discovered by the American psychologist Urie Bronfenbrenner (1961, 45–46), who was impressed that American and Russian images of each other, during the cold war, were symmetrical: "slowly and painfully, it forced itself upon me that the Russian's distorted picture of us was curiously similar to our view of them – a mirror image." I will get back to the "mirror image" in more detail in the next chapters.

27 Compare to Bar-Tal (1998) who claims implicitly that entrenched societal beliefs function in a similar manner to psychological defense mechanisms. On the one hand, they enable the continuation of the conflict. On the other hand, they help the society members to cope "successfully" with a situation of unending conflict.

28 Compare to Huntington ([1968] 2006, 3) who describes the collapse of the modernizing countries of Asia, Africa, and Latin America after World War II.

29 See Ottaway (1993, 10–11).

30 No doubt it is possible to continue describing the phenomenon of intractable conflict from many additional points of view. The critical question is: How to construct a sophisticated peacemaking strategy that could cope with such multidimensional complications?

31 See Mitchell (1999, 184).

32 See Bickerton and Klausner (2007, 219).

33 See Kelman (2001, 189).

34 For a further discussion upon the establishment of Hamas, see Abu-Amr (1993).

35 For a further discussion upon the human limitations of any social experts and its implications upon his or her work, see Hayek (1967).

36 See Kriesberg (1993), Bar-Tal (1998) and Coleman (2000).

2 The Palestinian-Israeli conflict

1 Senator Mitchell (1999, 28) describes how representatives of opposing factions presented the story of Northern Ireland to the President of the United States, Bill Clinton. Each representative presented the history of Northern Ireland from his own perspective. Each of the narratives, as Mitchell reported, were completely different and yet fascinating and persuasive.

2 In the Minds of Peace Experiment – a small Palestinian-Israeli public negotiating assembly – which is conducted around the United States, Canada, and the Middle East, the negotiators are instructed: to focus upon improving the present situation, to visualize a better future, and to make demands by peaceful means. I will get back to this peacemaking initiative in Chapter 7: The public-assembly model. To view a brief overview of the initiative and the agreements that each round achieved, visit http://mindsofpeace.org/.

3 For a comprehensive account of the history of the conflict see Bickerton and Klausner (2007) and Tessler (1994).

4 See, for example, Halpern (1969) and Hertzberg (1973).

5 For example, Leo Pinsker in his famous political pamphlet *Auto-Emancipation*, written in 1882, following the 1881 pogroms in Russia, emphasized the urgent necessity to build a state for the Jewish people in their historic fatherland.

6 See "The Basel Declaration" in Bickerton and Klausner (2007, 33).

7 The terms of the Arab revolt against the Turks during World War I were discussed with the British administration in the unofficial Hussein-McMahon correspondence in 1915 (the documents can be viewed in Bickerton and Klausner
2007, 55–57). The Arab led an uprising against the Turks under the impression
that it would lead to an independent Arab state which would include Palestine.
This was Arab wishful thinking that the British did not fulfill.

8 An example of the rise of Arab nationalism was the establishment of the Arab
League in Cairo in 1945.

9 Of course, the question who is a refugee is subject to dispute, debate, and negotiation. For example, people on both sides believe that the main focus should be
on Palestinians, who even now, experience the difficult conditions of living in
refugee camps in various locations, such as Lebanon. In any case, one version
of the "two state solution," which is the consensus solution to the Palestinian-
Israeli conflict, suggests that the refugees will be entitled compensation for loss
of property and will be granted the right to return to the new Palestinian state. To
view this proposal visit: http://www.geneva-accord.org/mainmenu/summary.

10 Pan-Arabism is often associated with Nasserism. For a further discussion, see
Podeh and Winckler (2004).

11 Kelman (1997, 184–86).

12 In the Cairo summit of 1964, the Arab League informed the Palestinians that they
have to assume responsibility for "liberating" Palestine (Bickerton and Klausner
2007, 141).

13 See, for example, "The Likud Response to Camp David" (the document can be
viewed in Bickerton and Klausner 2007, 201).

14 See, for example, "The Palestinian National Covenant" from 1968 (the document can be viewed in Bickerton and Klausner 2007, 173–75).

15 Already in 1974 the PLO leadership was willing to consider the establishment
of a Palestinian Arab state in Gaza and the West Bank. However, Israeli analysts
claimed that this was only a tactical move in a strategy that intended to pave the
way for the destruction of Israel (Bickerton and Klausner 2007,183).

16 For a further discussion about the tensions between state and church in Israel see
Agassi (1999).

17 For a further discussion upon the birth of the settlements see Aronson (1990).
I will get back to the settlement issue in Chapter 5: The social-reformer
model.

18 Arafat, who spoke before the UN General Assembly in 1974, was the first non-
state representative to deliver a speech in this forum. There are other factors
beside physical violence that attracted attention to the Palestinian problem, for
example, the dependency of western countries on Arab oil.

19 For a further discussion and a detailed overview of the establishment and nature
of Hamas, see Abu-Amr (1993). I will get back to the leadership struggle in
Palestinian society in Chapter 5: The social-reformer model.

20 See Agha *et al.* (2003, 35).

21 For comprehensive coverage and analysis of the Oslo Accord, see Agha *et al.*
(2003, 29–56). I will get back to the Oslo Accord in a more detailed analysis in
Chapter 6: The political-elite model.

22 To view the Oslo agreement, "The Israeli-PLO Declaration of Principles," see
Bickerton and Klausner (2007, 261–71).

23 Hamas won the majority of seats in the Palestinian parliamentary elections in

2006 while the President of the Palestinian authority, Mahmoud Abbas is a PLO member.

24 See "The Cabinet Resolution Regarding the Disengagement Plan, June 6, 2004, as Published by the Israeli Prime Minister's Office" in Bickerton and Klausner (2007, 380–83).

25 See, for example, Abu-Amr (1993, 12) and Bickerton and Klausner (2007, 223).

26 In the Annapolis conference in 2007, the President of the Palestinian authority, Mahmoud Abbas, and the Israeli Prime Minister, Ehud Olmert, articulated their commitment to a "two state solution." However, the Palestinian society was already divided. Hamas leadership in the Gaza strip led protests and demonstrations against the conference.
To view the conference's documents visit:
http://www.mfa.gov.il/MFA/History/Modern+History/Historic+Events/The+A nnapolis+Conference+27-Nov-2007.htm.

27 The "Minds of Peace Experiment" – a Palestinian-Israeli public negotiating assembly, which my colleagues and I have conducted around the US, Canada and the Middle East, support this observation. Only Palestinians who live in the Diaspora have brought the "one state solution" to the negotiating table, so far. There was no discussion upon the "one state solution" in the negotiations in Israel and Palestine. For further information about the "Minds of Peace Experiment" visit: http://mindsofpeace.org/. I will discuss the Minds of Peace Experiment and its practical implications further in Chapter 7: The public-assembly model.

28 The philosophers Karl Popper and Joseph Agassi pointed out that any search for solutions to complicated problems can quite easily slide to the margins (one state or two states). In order to avoid this trap they proposed an "opposite" methodology: first to demarcate the landscape of the discussion by presenting the extreme options and then to begin searching for a more realistic answer. As their student and follower, I am following this methodology here.

29 See, for example, Elazar (1991, 37):

> Federalism is most commonly perceived to be a matter of governmental structure involving two or more "units," "arenas," "planes," or "levels" of government, each endowed with a substantial degree of independence, full legitimacy, and a constitutionally guaranteed place in the overall system and possessing its own set of institutions, powers, and responsibilities, constitutionally linked within a common governing framework for specified purposes.

30 The idea of establishing a Palestinian-Israeli public negotiating congress is loosely based on the multi-party talks that helped to create a turning point in two other cases of intractable conflicts: Northern Ireland during the "troubles" and the struggle against the Apartheid in South Africa. Following the Good Friday Agreement in 1998, Northern Ireland's all-party talks were transformed into a political peacekeeping institution, known as the Northern Ireland Assembly.

3 Between conflict-resolution and conflict-management

1 Compare to Inbar (2006) and Landau (2006, 268).
2 Compare to Bar-Siman-Tov (2007, 9).

3 Inbar (2006) labels the Palestinian authority a failed state. However, the failure of the Palestinian authority to establish a decent modern state is not unique. The South African experience, as many other cases do, demonstrates that the first attempts to make a democratic transition are likely to fail and the failures can bring catastrophic results. See, for example, Huntington (1992, 597–98).
4 See Bronfenbrenner (1961).
5 Compare to Kelman (2007, 294–97).
6 Kelman (1981, 95–96), for example, associates the beginning of peace research with the emergence of the academic peace movement. The movement was established in 1952 by a group of scholars who joined efforts to explore possibilities to prevent wars and resolve international conflicts. No doubt many peace scholars will disagree with Kelman. But, it is beyond controversy that peace research is a new emerging profession in academia comparing to most classical academic disciplines, such as: mathematics, philosophy, and political science.
7 See, for example, Banks (1984, 20) and Fisher (1997, 1–2). Compare also to Hopmann (1995, 25) who claims that a systematic study of negotiation in International Relations started around 1960.
8 See, for example, Nye (2009, 220).
9 Compare to Allison (1971, 3):

>   . . . we are assuming governmental behavior can be most satisfactorily understood by analogy with the purposive acts of individuals. In many cases this is a fruitful assumption. Treating national governments as if they were a centrally coordinated, purposive individual provides a useful shorthand for understanding problems of policy.

10 There can be no doubt that one of the climaxes of the realist paradigm is manifested in *The Prince* written by Niccolo Machiavelli about 500 years ago. Machiavelli's answer to the situation of ongoing civil wars is a criminal autocrat. I present the logic behind Machiavelli's proposal and its practical implication in Chapter 4: The strong-leader model.
11 For a realist description and examination of the crisis and its resolution see Allison (1971), especially his analysis according to the Rational Actor Model (model 1).
12 See, for example, Thomas Schelling's (2005) Nobel Prize Lecture in http://nobelprize.org/nobel_prizes/economics/laureates/2005/schelling-lecture.pdf. Professor Schelling has inspired generations of strategic thinkers by pioneering "the study of strategic bargaining, which describes how states can exploit military, economic and other relative advantages to advance their interests through favorable bargaining outcomes." For a critical discussion upon the ethical aspects of Schelling's work see Lebow (2007, 255 – 77).
13 See Banks (1984, 19)
14 Compare to Fisher (1997, 6).
15 Another version of the anti-realist paradigm is "complex interdependence," as presented by Nye (2009, 220). Nye claims that realism and complex interdependence (anti-realism) are ideal types that can help us in sketching the spectrum of the political discussion. For example, the relationships between states can be viewed and analyzed as different combinations of realism and complex interdependence.
16 See Banks (1984, 20).

17 Scholars who have endorsed a pluralistic approach to the study of destructive social conflicts and their resolution, developed various methodological approaches to peacemaking and named them differently. For example, Burton named his version "control communication"; Fisher (1997) called his understanding of the peacemaking process "interactive conflict resolution"; Kelman (1996) labeled his approach "interactive problem solving workshop."

18 A main motive in the Jewish Israeli experience is an extreme fear for security. Anwar Sadat, the former President of Egypt, who was very sensitive and attentive to the public opinion in Israel, sophisticatedly approaches this issue. In his historic speech in the Israeli Parliament in 1977, the president continuously repeated that one of the meanings of peace is that Israel will receive the necessary guaranties for its security. For a comprehensive discussion upon this issue, see Chapter 4: The strong-leader model.

19 The academic umbrella enabled the representatives to begin the sessions with an open mind and to let go of the usual defenses that they are used to. It is quite clear that Burton's purpose exceeded far beyond a pure academic analysis of the sources of the conflict. As the rest of the sessions show, the main purpose was to explore a new method for conflict resolution. The meaning is that Burton employed manipulative elements for a benevolent cause. Indeed, social scientists have already noted that achieving an effective change in human behavior requires the application of manipulative elements. For a further discussion upon the ethical limits of manipulation, see Handelman (2009).

20 This is only a brief simplification of a complex reality. My intention is to show how a new approach to conflict resolution was born. For a more detailed description of the story see Fisher (1997, 21–23).

21 For example, the failed attempts to prepare the ground for resolving the conflict in Cyprus in 1966 by applying Burton's new methodology "control communication." For a further discussion upon the Cyprus meeting and its implication, see Fisher (1997, 25–26).

22 Kelman (1996, 99).

23 For a further discussion upon the differences and similarities between these two concepts of negotiation (bargaining versus problem solving), see Hopmann (1995).

24 A "failed state" is a term used to describe a failure of the central government to maintain law and order and meet the basic needs of the population. Inbar (2006) claimed that the Palestinian Authority, under Arafat's control, met the criteria for a failed entity. The dysfunction of the Palestinian Authority led to a civil war between Hamas and the PLO and a political division between Gaza and the West Bank.

25 Compare to Allison (1971, 4–5):

> . . . most analysts and ordinary laymen attempt to understand happenings in foreign affairs as the more or less positive acts of unified national governments. Laymen personify rational actors and speak of their aims and choices. Theorists of international relations focus on problems between nations in accounting for the choices of unitary rational actors . . . For each of these groups, the point of an explanation is to show how the nation or government could have chosen to act as it did, given the strategic problem it faced.

26 See Banks (1984, 19).

27 See Fisher (1997).

4 The strong-leader model

1 Ironically, Machiavelli, who proved his excellence in humanist studies, was chosen to serve as a diplomat at the age of 29. See Skinner (1981, 3–4).

2 For a further discussion upon the Machiavellian revolution in modern political philosophy, see Mannet (1996, 10–19) and Strauss (1989, 39–51).

3 For a different formulation of this question see Mansfield (1972, 102).

4 See Strauss (1989, 44–47) and Agassi (1985, 193).

5 Compare to Dietz (1986, 780).

6 See Wantchekon (2004).

7 See Hobbes ([1651] 1985) and Huntington ([1968] 2006).

8 This strategy often called "authoritarian transition." See Huntington ([1968] 2006, xiii).

9 Hayek F.A., interviews in *El Mercurio* (Santiago, Chile, 1981) from http://www.hayekcenter.org/takinghayekseriouslyarchive/005571.html.

10 This point arises many times in Machiavelli's text. See, for example, Machiavelli ([1532] 1979a: 153).

11 As it is well known, Niccolo Machiavelli by writing *The Prince*, an advice book for the common authoritarian leader, is considered as the thinker who turned the study of politics into an applied science. However, on the other hand, it is quite clear that no person has ever achieved a position of power and rulership by applying Machiavelli's suggestions and recommendations. For a further discussion see Silone (1938) and Handelman (2006).

12 See Machiavelli ([1532] 1979a, 165–66).

13 Compare to Strauss (1989, 42):

> The passion in question is the desire for glory. The highest form of the desire for glory is the desire to be a new prince in the fullest sense of the term, a wholly new prince: a discoverer of a new type of social order, a molder of many generations of men. The founder of society has a selfish interest in the preservation of society, of his work. He has therefore a selfish interest in the members of his society being and remaining sociable, and hence good.

14 In a Likud party referendum held in May 2004, about 60 percent of the participants voted against Sharon's disengagement plan.

15 See, for example, Hirst and Beeson, *Sadat* (1981, 252–54).

16 It seems that the fear and worry which are fundamental to the Jewish-Israeli essence were well known to the Egyptian President. Indeed, in his historical speech in the Israeli parliament, Sadat (1977) had repeated several times that every peace agreement will have to include guarantees to ensure security for Israel:

> What is peace for Israel? It means that Israel lives in the region with her Arab neighbors, in security and safety. To such logic, I say yes. It means that Israel lives within her borders, secure against any aggression. To such logic, I say yes. It means that Israel obtains all kinds of guarantees that ensure those two factors. To this demand, I say yes. More than that: we declare that we accept all the international guarantees you envisage and accept.

17 Sadat describes the situation well in his historical speech at the Israeli parliament on November 20, 1977:

I can see the point of all those who were astounded by my decision or those who had any doubts as to the sincerity of the intentions behind the declaration of my decision. No one would have ever conceived that the President of the biggest Arab State, which bears the heaviest burden and the top responsibility pertaining to the cause of war and peace in the Middle East, could declare his readiness to go to the land of the adversary while we were still in a state of war. Rather, we all are still bearing the consequences of four fierce wars waged within thirty years. The families of the 1973 October War are still moaning under the cruel pains of widowhood and bereavement of sons, fathers and brothers. As I have already declared, I have not consulted, as far as this decision is concerned, with any of my colleagues and brothers, the Arab Heads of State or the confrontation States. Those of them who contacted me, following the declaration of this decision, expressed their objection, because the feeling of utter suspicion and absolute lack of confidence between the Arab States and the Palestinian People on the one hand, and Israel on the other, still surges in us all. It is sufficient to say that many months in which peace could have been brought about had been wasted over differences and fruitless discussions on the procedure for the convocation of the Geneva Conference, all showing utter suspicion and absolute lack of confidence.

18 In this context, it seems important to pay attention that Sadat's historic speech is not absent of demagogic motifs. For example, he approaches the Israeli Jews and says: "you have to give up . . . the belief that force is the best method for dealing with the Arabs." Of course, such preaching does not come from a liberal ruler that respects the democratic rights of his people.

19 Bickerton and Klausner (2007, 190–91).

20 See, for example, Machiavelli ([1532] 1979a: 133):

How praiseworthy it is for a prince to keep his word and to live by integrity and not by deceit everyone knows; nevertheless, one sees from the experience of our times that the princes who have accomplished great deeds are those who have cared little for keeping their promises and who have known how to manipulate the minds of men by shrewdness; and in the end they have surpassed those who laid their foundations upon honesty.

21 Compare to the well-known philosopher of war Carl von Clausewitz's famous controversial quotation: "War is not a mere act of policy but a true political instrument, a continuation of political activity by other means." Or the Chinese military theorist Sun Tzu's famous maxim: "All is War."

22 See http://likud1.ios.st/Front/NewsNet/reports.asp?reportId = 29214.

23 See "The Cabinet Resolution Regarding the Disengagement Plan, June 6, 2004" in Bickerton and Klausner (2007, 380).

24 A good example is the Passover Haggada (text used on the festival meal which opens the Passover holiday).

25 For a further discussion see Bar-Tal (1998).

26 I am emphasizing "Jewish Israeli" because not every Jew is Israeli and not every Israeli is Jewish. Indeed, many Israelis are not Jewish. For a further discussion upon this issue see Agassi (1999).

27 For a more detail account of the power struggle within Palestinian society, see the next chapter.

28 For example, the Israeli cabinet resolution, regarding the derangement plan of June 6, 2004, concluded:

> The goal is that implementation of the plan will lead to improving the situation and breaking the current deadlock. If and when there is evidence from the Palestinian side of its willingness, capability and implementation in practice of the fight against terrorism, full cessation of terrorism and violence and the institution of reform as required by the Road Map, it will be possible to return to the track of negotiation and dialogue
>
> (Bickerton and Klausner, 2007, 383)

29 This is one of the major reasons that the social-reformer model, which is the topic of the next chapter, is so needed.

30 A similar phenomenon occurred after the assassination of the Israeli Prime Minister Yitzhak Rabin on November 1994. There is a common belief that Rabin was the only Israeli leader who would be able to save the Oslo peace process from collapsing. For a psychological explanation of the human being's desire for the emergence of a protective father (a strong leader) to solve our most daunting problems, see Freud ([1927] 1968). The art of peacemaking, according to this book, is to create an effective process that does not depend on one political leader or another.

31 See Kelman (1997, 184–85)

32 Carter described this peacemaking process as "one of the most frustrating experiences of my life" (Bickerton and Klausner 2007, 190).

33 The dramatic release of Nelson Mandela from prison, on February 1990, by Frederik Willem de Klerk, the last president of the Apartheid era in South Africa, is another example of a strong leader move. See Sparks (1994).

5 The social-reformer model

1 See, for example, Huntington ([1968] 2006) and Buchanan (2001).

2 For example in the St. Louis round of the Minds of Peace Experiment – a minor scale of Palestinian-Israeli public negotiating assembly – the two delegations used insights from the Geneva accord in their agreements. To view the agreements visit http://www.mindsofpeace.org/.

I will return to the experiment and its practical implications in Chapter 7: The public-assembly model.

3 For a further discussion, see for example, Caldwell (1977, 1867–68) and Handelman (2008).

4 It is not clear whether Israel, actually, supported the Muslim Brotherhood or simply did not interfere in their activity. The agenda of the Muslim Brotherhood was clear from the beginning: establishing an Islamic state, with the Quran and the *sunna* serving as guidance in all aspects of life, in the Holy Land. The Brotherhood preached and taught that sacrificing life and money for the liberation of the Holy Land (not only Gaza and the West Bank) is a religious obligation. For a further discussion upon establishment of Hamas and its relation to the Muslim Brotherhood, see Abu-Amr (1993).

5 I was inspired by Friedrich Hayek's (1978) perception of market competition. Hayek emphasizes that competition is a vehicle for innovations, elaborations and discoveries.

6 Hayek, especially in *The Constitution of Liberty* (Hayek, 1960), argues that a decent society should be conducted as a multidimensional free market. Accordingly, the economic sphere is only one dimension of the whole structure that enables cementing general claims about the decent social order.

7 For a clear presentation of this issue, see Heilbroner (1996: 40).

8 See, for example, Hayek ([1973] 1993, 154) and Handelman (2008, 109).

9 See, for example, Buchanan (2001) and Vanberg (2005, 25–26).

10 See, for example, Hayek ([1973] 1993, 45): "The question which is of central importance as much for social theory as for social policy is thus what properties the rules must possess so that the separate actions of the individuals will produce an overall order."

11 Compare to Huntington ([1968] 2006, xix): "Just as economic development depends, in some measures, on the relation between investment and consumption, political order depends in part on the relation between the development of political institutions and the mobilization of new social forces into politics."

12 See Mitchell (1999, 117).

13 Rabin, despite his extensive military record (Chief of Staff during the 1967 war), was disparaged personally and described as the enemy of Israel by right-wing extremists who opposed the process. Rallies where posters portrayed Rabin in a Nazi SS uniform make one wonder where exactly the boundary between legitimate democratic protest and illegitimate incitement is.

14 For a further discussion upon the unexpected victory of Benjamin Netanyahu, a right-wing hardliner, over Shimon Peres, a visionary peacemaker, see Handelman (2009, 89–91).

15 See Ottaway (1993, 10–11).

16 Huntington ([1968] 2006, 3).

17 See Popper ([1945] 1947).

18 See Aronson (1990).

19 Rubin (1999).

20 See Aronson (1990, 13).

21 Bickerton and Klausner (2007, 165).

22 See, for example, "The Basel Declaration" of the first Zionist Congress in Basel in 1897. The document can be found in Bickerton and Klausner (2007, 33).

23 The "Minds of Peace Experiment," a simulation of a potential Palestinian-Israeli public negotiating congress, demonstrates this observation quite well. Many times, it is the opinionated participants with more radical views who tend to lead their delegation towards a compromise that they usually objected to initally. For a further discussion, see Chapter 7: The public-assembly model.

24 See, for example, the Geneva accord, an Israeli-Palestinian initiative to end the conflict, in http://www.geneva-accord.org/.

25 Agassi (1999) claims that the right-wing extremists are the only Israeli political group that presents a clear strategy. Their political program, which includes different kinds of "transferring" Palestinian populations, is not acceptable in decent democracy. Agassi claims that in times of distress and pressure, people tend to embrace the most available strategy. Israel, according to Agassi, is marching toward a disaster without any political strategy and backup planning. The Jewish state can find itself coping with a state of emergency by adapting a political program that is certainly not in tune with Jewish morality and values.

26 Bickerton and Klausner (2007, 186).

27 Huntington (1992) noted that great leaders are those who succeed in establishing broad coalitions. The tragic events following the Israeli disengagement from Gaza in 2005 points that such political skill is not enough to gain greatness and glory.

28 Sharon failed to get the support of his own party on his proposal to unilaterally withdraw from the Gaza Strip. However, the stubborn Prime Minister ignored his loss in his own party referendum and carried out the disengagement plan.

29 Popper ([1945] 1947, 149–51), for example, noted that democracy is a political system that gives people the right to criticize their rulers and dismiss them without bloodshed.

30 See Bickerton and Klausner (2007, 223).

31 No doubt there are different versions of pan-Arabism and Islamism. Pan-Arabism is a set of political programs that center around the unity of the Arab world. For example, the Syrian Bath party, which was established in 1950, combined Arab unity with socialism, and its slogan became: "Arab freedom, Arab socialism, and Arab unity" (Bickerton and Klausner, 2007, 136). Pan-Islamism is set of ideologies emphasizing that Islam is a religious and political system. The Muslim Brotherhood is an example of an Islamist movement that seeks to establish an Islamic state as its political goal, with the Quran and the *sunna* serving as guidance for all aspects of life (Abu-Amr, 1993, 6).

32 Nasser's version of pan-Arabism is well known as Nasserism. For a further discussion, see, for example, Podeh and Winckler (2004).

33 The greatest achievement of the pan-Arabism movement, under the leadership of Nasser, is considered to be the creation of United Arab Republic (UAR) which was established in 1958 and survived until 1961. For a further discussion, see Bickerton and Klausner (2007, 136).

34 No doubt there are other major political events, such as the Islamic revolution in Iran in 1979, which contributed to the rise of radical Islam.

35 For a further discussion, see Kelman (1997, 184–85) who coined the term "Palestinization of the Arab-Israeli conflict."

36 For an historical overview of the evolution of the Muslim Brotherhood in the Palestinian territories, see Abu-Amr(1993, 5–8).

37 The original agenda of the Brotherhood was to prepare the conditions toward the establishment of pan-Islamic state (*Caliphate*) that would declare holy war (*jihad*) against Israel. Sheikh Ahmad Yassin, one of the leading members of the Brotherhood and one of the founding members of Hamas, changed this initial political program. Yassin insisted that the establishment of an Islamic state in Palestine, which would wage a holy war against Israel, is a necessary cornerstone in the road to establish a pan-Islamic state. For a further discussion, see Abu-Amr (1993, 10–12) and Bickerton and Klausner (2007, 223).

38 See Rubin (1999, 4–6).

39 See Abu-Amr (1993)

40 See, for example, Landau (2006, 261–63).

41 For an interesting discussion and radical proposal to solve this problematic issue, see Agassi (1999).

42 Landau (2006: 261–63) notes that many Arab-Israelis have family relatives among the Palestinians.

43 This is one of the reasons that so many people go to psychotherapy. For a further discussion, see Handelman (2009).

44 Anwar Sadat, the former President of Egypt, seemed to understand it very well.

However, there is a big difference between the Israeli-Egypt situation and the Israeli-Palestinian circumstances. I elaborated on this point in Chapter 4: The strong-leader model.
45 Compare to Popper ([1945] 1947).
46 In another place, I offered a dual strategy to cope with the Palestinian-Israeli struggle: conflict-management in the Israeli-Gaza situation and conflict-resolution in the Israeli-West Bank case. I named this duel strategy: "The Bangladesh Approach to the Palestinian-Israeli Struggle."

6 The political-elite model

1 See Agha *et al.* (2003: 1–3). Of course, there are other diplomatic channels of peacemaking that involve political-elite interactions, such as shuttle diplomacy. However, I find their importance to the current situation in the Palestinian-Israeli struggle less substantial.
2 Compare to Agha *et al.* (2003, 3) who distinguish between "soft" and "hard" Track II talks. The first is "aimed at an exchange of views, perceptions, and information between the parties to improve each side's understanding of the other's positions and policies." The second is designed to "help negotiate political agreements between governments."
3 For example, secrecy was necessary for the success of the Oslo Accord. However, the price was that the general public and important political-elites were kept out of the process. The results were the lack of appropriate public preparation to accept the emerging agreement and the full consequences of a continuing peace process. See Kelman (1997, 190).
4 The Palestinians, from their side, were interested to get to know the settlers, who were considered to be the most entrenched opponent to any solution which supports the establishment of a Palestinian independent state. The talks began with unofficial representatives; however, almost from the beginning, officials from the PLO and the Palestinian authority joined in. For a comprehensive description and analysis of the story, see Agha *et al.* (2003, 91–101).
5 Of course, there are additional reasons that made the talks less relevant, at least, to the Israeli settlers. For example, the 1996 victory of the Likud (the right-wing party) in the Israeli general elections and the ongoing suicide bombing inside Israel during that time. For a further discussion, see Agha *et al.* (2003, 95).
6 In 2005, about ten years later, the settlers led a massive campaign against Sharon's unilateral withdrawal from Gaza and gave the impression that the Israeli society was about to experience a civil war. The irony of fate is that Israel somehow survived the shock but Palestinian society faced a tragic civil war between Hamas (the radical Islamist movement) and Fatah (the secular party).
7 See Dayan (1981, 43).
8 For a further discussion upon those secret diplomatic missions, see Gilboa (1998, 213).
9 At the beginning of the twentieth century US President Woodrow Wilson named secret diplomacy as a major cause for the evils that led to World War I. The first of his Famous Fourteen Points, proclaimed in his famous speech on January 8, 1918, emphasizes the need for open diplomacy to maintain a peaceful social order: "Open covenants of peace, openly arrived at, after which there shall be no private international understandings of any kind but diplomacy shall pro-

ceed always frankly and in the public view." However, later, he emphasized that diplomacy does not necessarily mean negotiations but the results of negotiation. In other words, for the sake of peace it is sometimes necessary to negotiate secretly but agreements should not be remain hidden. For a further discussion, see De Magalhães (1988, 69).

10 See, for example, Hamilton and Langhorne (1995).
11 The unofficial exchange of letters, known as "Hussein–McMahon correspondence," can be seen in Bickerton and Klausner (2007, 55–57).
12 To see the agreement visit http://www.mideastweb.org/mesykespicot.htm.
13 Hopmann (1995)
14 Kelman (1996, 100).
15 Compare to Kelman (1997, 189–93) and Kriesberg (2001, 378).
16 Kriesberg (2001, 378) distinguishes between mediators with leverage – in our case the President of the United States in Camp David – and problem-solving facilitators – in our case the Norwegians in the primary stage of the Oslo Accord.
17 In peacemaking literature, classic track II diplomacy is supposed to include unofficial elites from both sides. Since the Palestinian delegation included officials, some scholars suggested labeling the Oslo talks as track 1.5 diplomacy. The important issue is that the first stage of the Oslo process (the unofficial talks) had almost all the important characteristics of track II meetings. They were secret, not obligatory, and mediated by a third party (Norwegians) that did not have any direct interest in the region. Compare to Agha *et al.* (2003, 2–3).
18 Compare to Agha *et al.* (2003, 41).
19 The Oslo agreement is open to many interpretations. The different interpretations and the lack of satisfactory mechanisms to solve disputes caused a lot of tensions. This was one of the many reasons that, eventually, led to the collapse of the process.
20 See Savir (1998).
21 Agha *et al.* (2003, 35)
22 The organization's financial supporters in the Persian Gulf suspended their funds because of Arafat's support of Saddam Hussein during the Gulf War. See Agha *et al.* (2003, 34) and Bickerton and Klausner (2007, 250).
23 Bickerton and Klausner (2007, 250–51).
24 Agha *et al.* (2003, 54) claim that "the Oslo talks can be considered 'the mother of all track II talks' in the Middle East."
25 Compare to Kelman (2007, 292) who claims that the disaster was that both Rabin and Arafat prepared a reserve option in case the process collapsed. My main point is that, in general, political leaders should not be trusted. Their ability to shape the foundations of a new social order is limited. Therefore, even, full commitment to a historic peacemaking task is not enough.
26 There is a lot of literature focused on why the Oslo peace process failed. I discuss one hypothesis that certainly does not give a complete picture. My main point is that the political-elite model, i.e. interactions between elites, cannot alone bring about a sustainable peace in the complicated situation of the Palestinian-Israeli struggle.
27 Compare to Popper ([1945] 1947, 158) who claimed that first attempts to solve complicated problems are doomed to failure. However, criticizing our failures helps to better understand the challenge at stake and improve our methods and strategies:

Take as an example a practical problem, such as learning to ride a bicycle or to play the violin. With the exception perhaps of a few geniuses, all those who do not yet understand the problem of riding a bicycle are likely to fail at their first attempts to solve it. And so are those who do not yet understand the problem of playing the violin. But after a few failures they may begin to appreciate where the difficulty lies: they will begin to understand the problem. For a problem is nothing but a difficulty. And to understand a problem is nothing but being aware of what this particular difficulty is like.

28 The architects of the Oslo peace process thought about instruments, such as a Joint Israeli-Palestinian Liaison Committee, for coordination and cooperation between the two sides. However, it was not enough to solve tensions and disputes.

7 The public-assembly model

1 Compare to Hayek (1967, 22–42).
2 Compare to Courtney *et al.* (2005, 277).
3 See Mitchell (1999, 20):

> Later, when I became well known in Northern Ireland, I was often stopped by strangers, on the street, in the airport, in restaurants. They almost always offered words of gratitude and encouragement: "Thank you, Senator." "God bless you." "We appreciate what you're doing." And then, always the fear: "But you're wasting your time. We've been killing each other for centuries and we're doomed to go on killing each other forever."

4 Of course, "violent struggle" is a broad concept that has different meanings for different people. For example, part of the Palestinian population views the occupation as a violent reality while part of the Israeli population regards it as a self-defense necessity. Therefore, the exact meaning of the term has to be negotiated at the beginning of the discussions in the public-assembly. In the "Minds of Peace Experiment," a simulation of a potential Palestinian-Israeli public assembly which was conducted in December 2008 in St. Louis, the compromise was formulated in a joint document – "Confidence Building Measures." To view the document, visit http://mindofpeaceexperiment.blogspot.com/ or http://mindsofpeace.org/.
5 I am constantly repeating that prophecy in the social sciences is impossible. Moreover, in all our simulations of a Palestinian-Israeli public-assembly (the "Minds of Peace Experiment") the participants reached agreements. However, my assumption is that in a major Palestinian-Israeli public-assembly it will be extremely difficult to reach agreements. Nevertheless, I am insisting that establishing a major Palestinian-Israeli public-assembly is critical for creating the foundation of a meaningful peace process. To view the agreements that the simulations produced, visit: http://mindofpeaceexperiment.blogspot.com/ or http://mindsofpeace.org/.
6 Compare to Popper ([1945] 1947).
7 See Agassi (1985).
8 Ironically, Benjamin Netanyahu's election slogan "Peres will divide Jerusalem," which helped him to reach the prime minister's seat in 1996, brought the issue of

Jerusalem to the forefront of the Israeli public discussion, at least for some time. This election slogan contributed to the view that the fate of Jerusalem can be negotiable. It was, probably, the unintended consequence of a negative election campaign. For a comprehensive discussion, see Handelman (2009, 89–91).

9 See, for example, the frustration of Senator Mitchell who led the peace process in Northern Ireland (Mitchell, 1999, 126).
10 See Sparks (1994, 130)
11 See Courtney and Shapiro (1995).
12 See McKittrick and McVea (2002).
13 See Mitchell (1999, 184).
14 Ibid:

> Within days of Omagh atrocity, the new dissident groups which had, until then, opposed the Good Friday Agreement, announced the cessation of violence. For the first time in thirty years, all the paramilitary organizations operating in Northern Ireland declared a cease fire or suspension of military operations.

15 See Mitchell (1999, 143–83)
16 See *http://www.haaretz.com/hasen/spages/1080267.html.*
17 See *http://www.commongroundnews.org/article.php?id = 25355&lan = en&sid = 0&sp = 0&isNew = 1.*
18 See Kelman (1997, 188).
19 For a further discussion see Handelman (2006).
20 See, for example, Inbar (2006, 823–42) and Landau (2006, 239–40).
21 For example, a Palestinian public opinion poll from March 13–15, 2008, shows that

> 66 percent support and 32 percent oppose the Saudi initiative, which calls for Arab recognition of and normalization of relations with Israel after it ends its occupation to Palestinian territories occupied in 1967 and after the establishment of a Palestinian state . . . But the findings show total lack of confidence in diplomacy with 80 percent saying that negotiations launched by the Annapolis conference will fail while only 14 percent believe it will succeed . . . Pessimism about diplomacy also leads people to search for alternative means to end the occupation with findings showing about two-thirds (64 percent) supporting the continued launching of rockets from the Gaza Strip against Israeli towns and cities such as Sderot and Ashkelon.
> See http://www.pcpsr.org/survey/polls/2008/p27e1.html.

22 Bronfenbrenner (1961, 45–56) coined the term.
23 See the Mitchell report of the Sharm el-Sheikh Fact-Finding Committee, 2001: http://www.al-bab.com/arab/docs/pal/mitchell1.htm.
24 I have borrowed the term "competitive pluralism" from Raz (1986).
25 It is well known that competition can be a powerful vehicle to progress. Moreover, as free-market economists emphasize, in a competitive environment the self-interest of individuals is channeled spontaneously for the benefit of society. However, competition also can be destructive. Constitutional economists argue that constructive competition can emerge only in a framework of rules and institutions. In this respect, the public assembly is an institution that encourages

the emergence of constructive competition. Hayek (1960) discusses and elaborates the benefits of competition, while Buchanan (2001) adds the constitutional framework which is necessary to create constructive competition.

26 For example, in 1996 the IRA (Irish Republican Army) declared a cease-fire. Gerry Adams, the President of Sinn Fein, (the political party associated with the IRA) committed to principles of democratic and peaceful methods of negotiation ("Mitchell Principles"). As a result, Sinn Fein joined the conclusive negotiations on the future of Northern Ireland. It was one of the turning points in the peace process. See Mitchell (1999, 107–19).

27 For example, Mitchell opened a report on a sex scandal, which was one of the infinite scandals that threatened to wreck the multi-party talks, by noting: "The talks were constantly threatened by violence; that was no surprise, given the history of Northern Ireland. But it was a surprise when the talks were threatened by sex." See Mitchell (1999, 90–95).

28 For example, most Israelis and Palestinians do not meet each other. In general, Israelis are not allowed to visit the disputed territories and vice versa. Palestinians are not allowed to go into Israel without special permission. There are very few places where people from both sides can meet each other (without special permission) and it is not always easy to organize it.

29 Courtney *et al.* (2005, 302) and Dixon (2002).

30 Sparks (1994, 156).

31 Courtney, *et al.* (2005, 301–2)

32 Sparks (1994, 156)

33 Ironically, Tony Blair was appointed official Envoy of the Quartet on the Middle East and George Mitchell is the Middle East envoy on behalf of the US. Both of them were key players in the Northern Ireland peace process.

34 There are many grassroots organizations, such as Parents Circle that are committed to further the culture of peace through people-to-people discussions. However, as far as I know, the Minds of Peace Experiment is the first attempt to suggest a framework for people-to-people negotiations. Some of the grassroots organizations helped us to organize the Minds of Peace Experiment in Israel/Palestine and to recruit the people in the delegations.

35 Our approach suggests looking at peacemaking as a discovery procedure. A process where the two communities, Israelis and Palestinians, discover, mostly by themselves, the road to build the foundations for a peaceful coexistence. Our approach helps to bypass the question who can be the "optimal impartial" third-party mediator.

36 Sometimes it takes the delegations three sessions out five to reach a preliminary agreement on confidence building measures and on the suspension of the violent struggle.

37 Compare to Kelman's (1996, 106) perception of a just solution to the conflict: "The search for a solution that addresses the fundamental needs and fears of both parties can be viewed as the operationalization of the quest for justice in this approach. To the extent that the solution is responsive to these needs and fears, it does justice to each party". Kelman's work focuses on problem solving workshops (a certain mode of track II diplomacy) as part of the negotiation process.

38 The informal engagements are very important and sometimes, even, critical. They create opportunities: to get to know each other, to develop personal relationships, to explain the different positions better, to explore possibilities to advance the

formal discussion, and to try to soften hardliners. For example, in the first round of the Experiment (St. Louis, December 2008) the informal sessions, which were conducted in a Palestinian restaurant and a private house, helped to conclude three valuable agreements: "Declarations of Principles," "Confidence Building Measures," and "Agreement on Borders and Jerusalem."

39 From an academic point of view, we found major difficulties in formulating criteria for failure. The fact that Palestinians and Israelis agree to participate in such a difficult venue is already a success. Professor Agassi, a well-known expert on the philosophy of science, noted that a "big failure" – a consensus among the participants that a particular round of the experiment failed – will help to determine criteria for failure.

40 Beit Jala, which is located in the West Bank, is one of the few places that Palestinians from the West Bank and Israelis can meet without receiving a special permission from the authorities.

41 In the first round in St. Louis, the third agreement, "agreement on borders and Jerusalem," was not signed by all delegates. In the UCI-Irvine rounds, the agreement that the two delegations reached was not signed. To view the agreements visit http://mindsofpeace.org/ or http:// mindofpeaceexperiment.blogspot.com/

42 No doubt there is a large gap between the positions of the two delegations. It appears that tiredness from fighting and a strong desire to end the conflict are the main motives that led the delegations to reach compromises and conclude the agreements.

43 Each one of these models cannot sustain a lasting peace process by itself alone. I categorize the political-elite and the public-assembly as conflict resolution models because negotiations on multiple levels is a central element in each one of them.

44 The correlation between the development of knowledge and the ability to examine reality from different perspectives appears in many fields. For example, the well-known psychologist Jean Piaget associated the development of intelligence with the growing capability to examine the world from different angles of vision. Or, in the history of science it is quite common to view developments in modern physics as byproducts of examining old problems from additional perspectives (for example, Newtonian physics versus Einsteinian physics). For a further discussion, see for example, Holmes (1976).

45 I elaborate on this issue in Chapter 2: The Palestinian-Israeli conflict.

46 In general, federalism means configuration of diversity and unity. To put it differently, federalism means a structure involving separate independent unities "constitutionally linked within a common governing framework for specified purposes." For a further discussion, see Elazar (1991, 37).

Summary and conclusion

1 Compare to Hayek (1967) and Popper ([1945] 1947).

2 An example of non-violent principles of negotiation is the six ground rules regarding participation in the all-party talks on the future of Northern Ireland. These rules were formulated in 1996 and are known as the "Mitchell principles" (Mitchell, 1999, 35–36):

> To reach an agreed political settlement and to take the gun out of Irish politics, there must be commitment and adherence to fundamental principles of

democracy and non-violence. Participants in all-party negotiations should affirm their commitment to such principles.

Accordingly, we recommend that the parties to such negotiations affirm their total and absolute commitment:

- To democratic and exclusively peaceful means of resolving political issues;
- To the total disarmament of all paramilitary organizations;
- To agree that such disarmament must be verifiable to the satisfaction of an independent commission;
- To renounce for themselves, and to oppose any effort by others, to use force, or threaten to use force, to influence the course or the outcome of all-party negotiations;
- To agree to abide by the terms of any agreement reached in all-party negotiations and to resort to democratic and exclusively peaceful methods in trying to alter any aspect of that outcome with which they may disagree; and,
- To urge that "punishment" killings and beatings stop and to take effective steps to prevent such actions.

It is interesting to compare the "Mitchell principles," composed and approved by professional politicians, to the agreements that ordinary Palestinians and Israelis reached in the different rounds of the Minds of Peace Experiment (a small-scale Palestinian-Israeli public negotiating congress). For example, in the first round – which was conducted in the University of Missouri-St. Louis in December 2008 – the two delegations reached the following preliminary agreement:

We, the undersigned representatives of the following two Delegations, agree to the following principles:

1. That both the Palestinians and the Israelis have the right to self-determination; specifically, that Israel has a right to exist as a sovereign nation within secure, internationally recognized borders, and that Palestine has a right to exist as a sovereign nation within secure, internationally recognized borders.
2. That we will work toward a peaceful resolution of the Palestinian-Israeli conflict, with the understanding that the resolution we will achieve will represent a permanent solution to the conflict and the end of all grievances and demands between the two nations.
3. That we will suspend violence, violent struggle and incitement, in which (1) violence is defined as: unlawful use of physical force, as defined by international law, specifically, but not limited to, the Hague Regulations of 1907 and the Fourth Geneva Convention of 1949, exerted for the purpose of harming, violating, damaging, or abusing people; (2) violent struggle is defined as: political struggle that uses violence to achieve its objectives; and (3) incitement to violence is defined as: provoking or urging others to commit violence, using means that include, but are not limited to, public speeches, textbooks, television programming, and any act that would inherently cause humiliation.

4. In the event that an act of violence is committed by members of either nation, that we will unequivocally condemn the violence; that we will not halt the negotiation process despite the act of violence; and that we will ask the authority of the side that committed the act to take the necessary steps to capture and imprison perpetrators of violence who have acted unlawfully.
    The document can be found at: http://mindofpeaceexperiment.blogspot.com/2009/02/round-one-agreements_21.html

3   There can be no doubt that Anwar Sadat's diplomatic offensive in 1977 was a turning point in the Arab-Israeli conflict. However, this is a unique example. Usually, dramatic initiatives of strong political leaders are not enough to create such a substantial peacemaking effect, especially in situations of protracted social conflict where ordinary people are at the center of the struggle.

4   See Sparks (1994, 101).

5   See Mitchell (1999, 131–32).

6   The climax of the American civil rights struggle between 1955 and 1965 was the passage of the Civil Rights Act of 1964 and the Voting Rights Act of 1965 which ended the codification of racism in the United States; The Peace process in Northern Ireland culminated with the Good Friday Agreement of 1998 – a power-sharing agreement that concluded many years of sectarian violence (Mitchell 1999, 184–88); The struggle for change in South Africa led to the dismantling of the Apartheid system and transformation to democracy in 1994 (Sparks 1994, 226–40).
    The remarkable political transformation of these conflicts does not diminish how the transition process remains incomplete in each case. There remains much work to be done in order to improve socio-political conditions.

7   Sharon's unilateral withdrawal from Gaza and some territories in the West Bank in 2005 created a dramatic change in the geopolitical structure of the conflict. However, the progress and transformation, so far, is not in the direction of peace and reconciliation.

8   Shimon Peres, who became the Prime Minister of Israel after the assassination of Yitzhak Rabin in 1995, is considered to be a visionary peacemaking leader. Following the Oslo Accord, Peres often used to describe a vision of a new Middle East. His vision was not in tune with the ongoing suicide bombing inside Israel. Accordingly, a major part of the Israeli population saw Peres' vision as an unrealistic utopia. The results were that Peres lost the 1996 Israeli general election to Benjamin Netanyahu, who was considered to be an advocate of a pragmatic hard-line policy. For a further discussion upon the shift in Israeli politics, see Handelman (2009, 83–99).

9   Compare to Mitchell (1999, 186–88) who describes the reasons that led the people in Northern Ireland to endorse the Good Friday Agreement:

> The entire society learned from its mistakes. They learned that violence won't solve their problems, it will only make them worse. They learned that unionists and nationalists have more things in common than they have differences. They learned that knowledge of their history is a good thing but being chained to the past is not. Finally, they came to believe – with good reason – that peace and political stability will enable them to enjoy unprecedented growth and stability . . . when the people voted on May 1998, they knew what they were voting on. They might have disagreed with a detail

here and a provision there, but they understood that they were voting for peace, for tolerance, for mutual respect. Most of all, they were voting for their children, for a future not filled with fear and anxiety, not marked by random, senseless death . . . The people of Ireland are sick of war. They are sick of sectarian killings and random bombings. They are sick of the sad elegance of funerals, especially those involving the small white coffins of children, prematurely laid into the green fields of the Irish countryside. They want peace.

10 In most rounds of the Minds of Peace Experiment, demand for domestic reforms has been a key issue in the negotiating process and the agreements. To see the agreements, visit http://mindsofpeace.org/.
11 The Good Friday Agreement, which grew out of the all-party negotiations, created new democratic institutions to provide self-governance to Northern Ireland and to encourage cooperation between the north and south: "a Northern Ireland Assembly, to restore to the people the fundamental democratic right to govern themselves; and a North/South Council, to encourage cooperation and joint action for mutual benefit." (Mitchell 1999, 181) The Northern Ireland Assembly has been suspended on several occasions but the violent struggle was not renewed.
12 See, For example, Abu-Amr (1993).
13 For example, in the 2007 Annapolis conference, the Israeli Prime Minister Ehud Olmert and Palestinian President Mahmoud Abbas committed to a two state solution. Visit: http://www.guardian.co.uk/world/2007/nov/27/israel.usa1.
14 It is impossible to predict the outcomes of the dual approach: one, two, or, even, three states. This strategy is designed to help build the foundations of a peaceful social order according to the logic of the tragic circumstances.

Bibliography

Abu-Amr, Z. (1993) 'Hamas: A Historical and Political Background', *Journal of Palestine Studies*, 22 (4): 5–19.

Agassi, J. (1985) *Technology: Philosophical and Social Aspects*, Dordrecht, Holland: D. Reidel Publishing Company.

—— (1999) *Liberal Nationalism for Israel: Towards an Israeli National Identity*, Jerusalem and New York: Gefen Pub. House.

Agha, H., Feldman, S., Khalidi, A. and Schiff, Z. (2003) *Track-II Diplomacy: Lessons from the Middle East*, Cambridge, MA: MIT Press.

Allison G. (1971) *Essence of Decision: Explaining the Cuban Missile Crisis*, Boston: Little, Brown and Company.

Aronson, G. (1990) *Israel, Palestinians, and the Intifada: Creating Facts on the West Bank*, London and New York: Kegan Paul International in association with the Institute for Palestine Studies Washingon, D.C.

Banks, M. (1984) 'The Evolution of International Relations Theory' in M. Banks (ed.) *Conflict in World Society: A New Perspective in International Relations*, Sussex: Wheatsheaf books: 3–21.

Bar-Siman-Tov, Y. (2007) 'Dialectic between Conflict Management and Conflict Resolution' in Y. Bar-Siman-Tov (ed.) *The Israeli–Palestinian Conflict: From Conflict Resolution to Conflict Management*, New York: Palgrave Macmillan.

Bar-Tal, D. (1998) 'Societal Beliefs in Times of Intractable Conflict: The Israeli Case', *International Journal of Conflict Management*, 9 (1): 22–50.

Baron, H. (1961): 'Machiavelli: The Republican Citizen and the Author of *The Prince*', *English Historical Review*, 76 (299): 217–53.

Bickerton, Ian J. and Carla L. Klausner (2007) *A Concise History of the Arab-Israeli conflict, Fifth edition*, Englewood Cliffs, NJ: Prentice Hall.

Bronfenbrenner, U. (1961) 'The Mirror Image in Soviet-American Relations: A Social Psychologist's Report', *Journal of Social Issues* 17 (3): 45–56.

Buchanan, J. M. (2001) *Moral Science and Moral Order*. Vol. 17 of *The Collected Works of James M. Buchanan*, Indianapolis: Liberty Fund.

Caldwell, B. (1977) 'Hayek and Socialism', *Journal of Economic Literature* 35 (December): 1856–90.

Coleman, Peter T. (2000) 'Intractable Conflict' in M. Deutsch and P. T. Coleman (eds) *The Handbook of Conflict Resolution: Theory and Practice*, San Francisco: Jossey-Bass Publishers: 428–50.

Courtney, J. and Shapiro, I. (1995) 'South Africa's Negotiated Transition: Democracy, Opposition, and the New Constitutional Order', *Politics and Society* 23 (3): 269–308.

Courtney, J., Lust-Okar, E. and Shapiro, I. (2005) 'Problems and Prospects for Democratic Settlements: South Africa as a Model for the Middle East and Northern Ireland?', *Politics and Society* 33 (2): 277–326.

Dayan, M. (1981) *Breakthrough: A Personal Account of the Egypt-Israel Peace Negotiations*, London: Weidenfeld and Nicolson.

De Magalhães, J. C. (1988) *The Pure Concept of Diplomacy*, Connecticut: Greenwood Press.

Dietz, M. G. (1986) 'Trapping The Prince: Machiavelli and the Politics of Deception', *The American Political Science Review*, 80 (3): 777–99.

Dixon, P. (2002) 'Political Skills or Lying and Manipulation? The Choreography of the Northern Ireland Peace Process', *Political Studies*, 50 (3): 725–41.

Elazar, D. Y. (1991) *Two Peoples – OneLland: Federal Solutions for Israel, the Palestinians, and Jordan*, Lanham, MD: University Press of America.

Fisher, R. J. (1997) *Interactive Conflict Resolution*, New York: Syracuse University Press.

Freud S. ([1927] 1968) 'The Future of an Illusion' in *The Standard Edition of the Complete Psychological Works of Sigmund Freud,* 21: 3 – 56, Translated by James Strachey. London: Hogarth Press.

—— ([1933] 1968) 'Why War?' in *Civilisation, War and Death: 82-97.* Edited by John Rickman. London: Hogarth Press.

Gilboa, E. (1998) 'Secret Diplomacy in the Television Age', *Gazette: The International Journal for Communication Studies*, 60 (3): 211–25.

Halpern, B. (1969) *The Idea of a Jewish State,* Second edition, Cambridge, MA: Harvard University Press.

Hamilton, K. and Langhorne, R. (1995) *The Practice of Diplomacy,* London: Routledge.

Handelman, S. (2006) 'Between Machiavellian Leaders and the Arab–Israeli Conflict: Toward an Indirect Approach to Conflict Resolution in the Palestinian-Israeli Conflict', *Orient* 47 (4): 554–67.

—— (2008) 'Between *The Prince* and *The Road to Serfdom*: Two Political Pamphlets that Challenged the Conventional Wisdom of their Times', *Divinatio*, 28 (autumn-winter): 101–18.

—— (2009) *Thought Manipulation: The Use and Abuse of Psychological Trickery,* Santa Barbara, California: ABC-CLIO.

—— (2010) 'The Minds of Peace Experiment: A Simulation of a Potential Palestinian-Israeli Public Assembly', *International Negotiation: A Journal of Theory and Practice,* 15: 511–28.

—— (forthcoming) 'The Bangladesh Approach to the Palestinian-Israeli struggle: A Desperate Strategy to Cope with a State of Emergency,' *International Journal of Conflict Management.*

Hayek, F. A. (1960) *The Constitution of Liberty*, Chicago: The University of Chicago Press.

—— (1967) *Studies in Philosophy, Politics and Economics*, Chicago: University of Chicago Press.

—— [1973](1993) *The Political Order of a Free People. Volume 3 of Law, Legislation and Liberty*, London: Routledge and Kegan Paul.

—— (1978) 'Competition as a Discovery Procedure' in *New Studies in Politics, Philosophy, Economics and the History of Ideas*, Chicago: University of Chicago Press.

Heilbroner, R. L. (1996) *The Worldly Philosophers: The lives, Times and Ideas of The Great Economic Thinkers*, New York: Simon & Schuster.

Hertzberg, A. (1973), *The Zionist Idea*, New York: Atheneum.

Hirst, D. and Beeson, I. (1981) *Sadat*, London: Faber and Faber.

Hobbes, T. [1651] (1985), *Leviathan*, R. Tuck. (ed.) Cambridge: Cambridge University Press.

Holmes, R. (1976) *Legitimacy and the Politics of the Knowable*, London: Routledge.

Hopmann, P.T. (1995) 'Two Paradigms of Negotiation: Bargaining and Problem Solving', *The ANNALS of the American Academy of Political and Social Science*, 542 (1): 24–47.

Huntington, S. ([1968] 2006) *Political Order in Changing Societies*, New Haven, CT: Yale University Press.

—— (1992) 'How Countries Democratize', *Political Science Quarterly*, 106 (4): 579–616.

—— (1993) 'The Clash of Civilizations', *Foreign Affairs*, 72 (3): 22–49.

Inbar, E. (2006), 'Israel's Palestinian Challenge', *Israel Affairs*, 12 (4): 823–42.

Kelman, H. (1981) 'Reflections on the History and Status of Peace Research', *Conflict Management and Peace Science*, 5(2): 95–110.

—— (1996) 'Negotiation as Interactive Problem Solving', *International Negotiation: A Journal of Theory and Practice*, 1 (1): 99–123.

—— (1997) 'Some Determinants of the Oslo Breakthrough', *International Negotiation*, 2 (2): 183–94.

—— (2001) 'The Role of National Identity in Conflict Resolution: Experiences from Israeli-Palestinian Problem-solving Workshops', in R.D. Ashmore, L. Jussim, and D. Wilder (eds) *Social Identity, Intergroup Conflict, and Conflict Reduction* (187–212), Oxford and New York: Oxford University Press.

—— (2007) 'The Israeli-Palestinian Peace Process and its Vicissitudes: Insights from Attitude Theory', *American Psychologist* 63 (4): 287–303.

Kriesberg, L. (1993) 'Intractable Conflicts', *Peace Review*, 5 (4): 417–21.

—— (2001) 'Mediation and Transformation of the Israeli-Palestinian Conflict', *Journal of Peace Research* 38 (3): 373–92.

Landau, F. S. (2006) 'Settings, Factors and Phenomena of Conflict in the Israeli Society' in H., Albrecht, J., Simon, H., Rezaei, H., Rohne, E., Kiza (eds), *Conflicts and Conflict Resolution in Middle Eastern Societies – Between Tradition and Modernity*, Berlin: Duncker and Humblot.

Lebow R. (2007) *Coercion, Cooperation, and Ethics in International Relations*, New York : Routledge.

Machiavelli, N. [1531] (1979a) *The Discourses*, in P. Bondanella and M. Musa (ed.) *The Portable Machiavelli*. USA: Penguin Books.

—— [1532] (1979b) *The Prince*, in P. Bondanella and M. Musa (ed.) *The Portable Machiavelli*, USA: Penguin Books.

Mannet, P. (1996) *An Intellectual History of Liberalism*, R. Balinski (trans.) Princeton: Princeton University Press.

Mansfield, H. (1972): 'Necessity in the Beginnings of Cities' in A. Parel (ed.) *The Political Calculus*, Toronto and Buffalo: University of Toronto Press.

McKittrick, D., and McVea, D. (2002) *Making Sense of the Troubles: the Story of the Conflict in Northern Ireland*, Chicago: New Amsterdam Books.

Mitchell, G. (1999) *Making Peace*, New York, NY: Alfred A. Knopf.

Nye, J. (2009) *Understanding International Conflicts: An Introduction to Theory and History, Seventh edition*, New York: Pearson Longman.

Ottaway, M. (1993) *South Africa: The Struggle for a New Order*, Washington, D.C.: The Brookings Institution.

Pocock, J. G. A. (1975) *The Machiavellian Moment*, Princeton: Princeton University Press.

Podeh E. and Winckler O. (2004) *Rethinking Nasserism: Revolution and Historical Memory in Modern Egypt*, Gainesville: University Press of Florida.

Popper, K. ([1945] 1947): *The Open Society and its Enemies (vol. 2)*, London: Routledge.

—— ([1994] 1997) 'Models, Instruments and Truth', in M. A. Notturno (ed.) *The Myth of the Framework: In Defense of Science and Rationality*, London and New York: Routledge.

Raz, J. (1986) *The Morality of Freedom*, Oxford University Press.

Rigby, J. H. (1977) *Florence and the Medici*, London: Thames and Hudson.

Rubin, B. (1999) *The Transformation of Palestinian Politics: From Revolution to State – Building*, Cambridge, MA: Harvard University Press.

Russell, B. (2005) *History of Western Philosophy*, London and New York: Routledge.

Sadat, A. (1977): 'Statement to the Knesset by President Sadat', special meeting of the Knesset: the forty-third meeting of the ninth Knesset, (20 November 1977), Jerusalem.

Savir, U. (1998) *The Process: 1,100 Days that Changed the Middle East*, New York: Random House.

Silone, I. (1938) *The School for Dictators*, New York and London: Harper & Brothers Publishers.

Skinner, Q. (1981) *Machiavelli*, Oxford: Oxford University Press.

Smith, A. [1776] (1976) *An Inquiry into the Nature and Causes of the Wealth of Nations*, Chicago: University of Chicago Press.

Sparks, A. (1994) *Tomorrow Is Another Country: The Inside Story of South Africa's Negotiated Revolution*, Sandton, South Africa: Struik Book Distributors.

Strauss, L. (1989) *An Introduction to Political Philosophy, Detroit*: Wayne State University Press.

Sundquist, E. J. (2005) *Strangers in the Land: Blacks, Jews, Post-Holocaust America*, Cambridge, MA: Harvard University Press.

Tessler, M. (1994) *A History of the Israeli-Palestinian Conflict,* Bloomington and Indianapolis: Indiana University press.

Vanberg, V. (2005) 'Market and State: The Perspective of Constitutional Political Economy', *Journal of Institutional Economics* 1 (1): 23–49.

Wantchekon, L. (2004) 'The Paradox of "Warlord" Democracy: A Theoretical Investigation', *American Political Science Review*, 98 (1): 17–32.

Index

eBooks – at www.eBookstore.tandf.co.uk

A library at your fingertips!

eBooks are electronic versions of printed books. You can store them on your PC/laptop or browse them online.

They have advantages for anyone needing rapid access to a wide variety of published, copyright information.

eBooks can help your research by enabling you to bookmark chapters, annotate text and use instant searches to find specific words or phrases. Several eBook files would fit on even a small laptop or PDA.

NEW: Save money by eSubscribing: cheap, online access to any eBook for as long as you need it.

Annual subscription packages

We now offer special low-cost bulk subscriptions to packages of eBooks in certain subject areas. These are available to libraries or to individuals.

For more information please contact webmaster.ebooks@tandf.co.uk

We're continually developing the eBook concept, so keep up to date by visiting the website.

www.eBookstore.tandf.co.uk